Everyday
Genesis

Everyday Genesis

INVITING GOD
TO RE-CREATE YOU

Nika Maples

WORTHY®
PUBLISHING

Published by Worthy Books, an imprint of Worthy Publishing Group, a division of Worthy Media, Inc., One Franklin Park, 6100 Tower Circle, Suite 210, Franklin, TN 37067.

WORTHY is a registered trademark of Worthy Media, Inc.

HELPING PEOPLE EXPERIENCE THE HEART OF GOD

eBook available wherever digital books are sold.

Library of Congress Cataloging-in-Publication Data

Names: Maples, Nika, author.
Title: Everyday Genesis : inviting God to re-create you / Nika Maples.
Description: Franklin, TN : Worthy Publishing, 2017.
Identifiers: LCCN 2017020342 | ISBN 9781617956669 (tradepaper)
Subjects: LCSH: Christian life. | Bible. Genesis, II-II--Criticism, interpretation, etc.
Classification: LCC BV4501.3 .M2573 2017 | DDC 248.4--dc23
LC record available at https://lccn.loc.gov/2017020342

For foreign and subsidiary rights, contact rights@worthypublishing.com

ISBN: 978-1-61795-666-9

Cover Design: Kent Jensen | Knail
Interior Design and Typesetting: Bart Dawson

Printed in the United States of America
17 18 19 20 21 VPI 8 7 6 5 4 3 2 1

To Clint McDowell
1 Samuel 9:6

Contents

The Sixth Day, Morning

The Sixth Day, Afternoon

The Seventh Day

It stands to reason, doesn't it, that if the alive-and-present
God who raised Jesus from the dead moves into your life,
he'll do the same thing in you that he did in Jesus,
bringing you alive to himself?

—

ROMANS 8:11 MSG

Therefore, if anyone is in Christ, he is a new creation;
old things have passed away;
behold, all things have become new.

—

2 CORINTHIANS 5:17 NKJV

Altars of Earth

NEW HABITS FIND HARD GROUND to grow in me. At least, good ones do. Bad habits are brambles that choke back the change I want to make.

I have dropped my cell phone in a toilet six times, which is the number of times I have joined Weight Watchers, which is the number of times I have received speeding tickets (ahem, in the last *two* years alone . . .). I started biting my nails when I was three years old, and stopping it has topped my New Year's resolution lists ever since. When I turned thirty and my teeth started chipping as a result of the nail biting, I still didn't—even *couldn't*—change.

No self-help book, no motivating speaker, no special method has ever assisted me in quitting what I want to stop or beninning what I want to start. No tip or technique has done the trick. What does it mean if you don't stop things you hate? What does it mean if you don't start things you love? I am a writer, for instance, and I like writing. I relish how I feel while I am in the process of writing and also how I feel after I have written something meaningful. But I don't enjoy how I feel *before* I start writing, which is something like the continent of Africa. I feel huge and immovable. I always tell myself that I would be writing if only I had time, but then I actually set aside a period of time, and find myself resisting all the more. I look at that beckoning desk and become stiff-necked and defiant, wanting to *feel* ready before I come anywhere near the task. I cannot seem to roll my boulder body over to a chair to humbly sit. That's all I have to do.

Sit.

In a chair. In front of a computer. That's it.

Once I am in that magical position—ninety-degree knees, fingers on keys—I have no problem. The difficulty isn't the writing; it's that infernal chair. I don't like the way it shrugs at me, arms akimbo, as if to say, "Well, books don't write themselves, Nika. Are you going to do something about that today, or aren't you?"

That is the crux of it: if I sit down, I will have to *do* something. My brain will have to make words, and I wonder if I'll be able to do it this time. So, on a day when I have an empty afternoon, I become a nomad in my own home, sitting on the edge of the bed to eat lunch or on the rim of the bathtub to read mail. I perch.

No, I don't want to sit in a chair. Not in a chair that is too hard, not in a chair that is too soft, and not in a chair that is just right. This Goldilocks would rather wash a load of towels or organize the cans in the pantry or hand-chip ice for a homemade sno-cone than position herself to work on her real work.

I need a better tool, I tell myself, making another excuse. *I can't be the* only *writer who is looking for a motivational gimmick of some kind. Someone has to have thought of something that accelerates the process by now. I want an internal combustion engine for my mind. I want rocket fuel.*

I read once that Jerry Seinfeld advises would-be comedians

to use a red Sharpie and an enormous calendar to mark off the days they've attended to the creative task of writing new material. Eventually, they will bank up a crimson chain of days, even weeks.

"Don't break the chain!" he says.[1]

This seemed like a great idea, just checking off the dates with a marker and a calendar. It didn't work for me, though. As soon as I got a series of days going, I would look at that chain and *want* to break it. I'd *have* to break it, in fact, just to be sure I still had my freedom.

See? Tool after self-help tool has failed me.

Or I've failed them. Either way.

From overeating to speeding, I have found it impossible to re-make myself, and these are only the *bad habits* I've tried to convert into good ones; I haven't yet mentioned the *sins* I've tried to spin into righteousness. I haven't yet shared the jealousy I've learned to justify and the contempt I've tried to cover up.

Over time, I began feeling I was stuck being . . . me.

But there was something off about that idea. Now I react to this thought in my mind the same way I do when I read or hear other popular phrases among people in the church today. Phrases like "I am just a mess."

It sounds humble enough, but let's play the whole thing out: *I have given my life to Jesus, and yet I am still, in most ways, stuck. Broken. A mess.*

See? It just doesn't work.

It *almost* makes sense when I hear people sharing these self-deprecating evaluations. We want to stay modest and real, not giving off the foul odor of being "holier than thou." We want to avoid the stench of hypocrisy. But things make so much less sense when Christians use these descriptions. What we are saying, in-directly, when we call ourselves a mess, is that Jesus did quite a lot for us when He died on the cross and rose from the dead, but perhaps not enough. Crucifixion couldn't fix us. Alas, we're still broken.

And we're still advertising that we are.

I can hear someone saying, "Jesus is not the problem. His sacrifice was sufficient. It's *me* who can't seem to get it together." This person has seen the grace of Jesus, but has not taken hold of it. He accepts the gift of eternal life in heaven, but still ignores the gift of abundant life here on earth. He agrees that Christ took on the punishment of *death*, but still thinks he can handle the *life* part on his own.

I know because I have been that person. After all, Jesus has catastrophes and global starvation to tend to. I would hate to bother Him with my fingernails. I should be able to handle *that* much.

And so we kneel before the cross, giving Jesus our lives but not our living, and then we stand up and walk home to our occasional overdrinking and our it's-not-really-a-problem pornography. We return to our fractured relationships and our embarrassingly cluttered houses. We wear T-shirts that read, *I love Jesus, but I cuss a little.* For some reason we have believed that the initial decision to follow Christ would empower us to go back to our everyday lives and clean up the messes ourselves.

Eventually. But probably not today.

What is all this saying to the world? Who would ever want to become a Christian if, after embracing the blood of Christ, they were going to stay the messes they'd always been?

"Come follow Jesus," our lives say, "although you'll still have issues afterward, and, in fact, you'll have much more to do because you'll have to go to church and read the Bible and monitor your alcohol intake and avoid sexual temptation and be in a small group. This is on top of your current concerns, career responsibilities, and hectic schedule. Oh, by the way, you'll also be taken for an irrelevant rube by the general population. Good luck."

"Thanks but no," the world answers, rolling their eyes and walking away. Intelligent people don't decide to start seeing a doctor whose patients aren't getting any better.

Wait, Jesus interrupts. *Don't you know why I've come?* He says, "Healthy people don't need a doctor—sick people do. I have come to call not those who think they are righteous, but those who know they are sinners and need to repent."[2]

The Message puts it this way: "Who needs a doctor: the healthy or the sick? I'm here inviting outsiders, not insiders—an invitation to a changed life, changed inside and out."[3]

The evidence of a life lived with Jesus is change. Inside and out. The evidence is healing. Our Great Physician came to make us well. And that is not all.

Read Jesus's job description in Isaiah 61:1–3 (emphasis mine):

The Spirit of the Sovereign LORD is on me,
> because the LORD has anointed me
> to proclaim *good news* to the poor.
He has sent me to *bind up* the brokenhearted,
> to proclaim *freedom* for the captives
> and *release from darkness* for the prisoners,
to proclaim the year of the LORD's *favor*
> and the *day of vengeance* of our God,
to *comfort* all who mourn,
> and *provide* for those who grieve in Zion—
to bestow on them a crown of *beauty*
> instead of ashes,
the oil of *joy*
> instead of mourning,

and a garment of *praise*
     instead of a spirit of despair.

Isaiah 61 *was* Jesus's job description. But then He did it. And He said, "It is finished."[4] So now Isaiah 61 is Jesus's resume. It is no longer what He came to do. It is what He did.

It doesn't make sense that we would stay messes when Jesus has a curriculum vitae that sounds like the infomercial of our dreams: "He brings good news, but wait! There's more! Follow Jesus now and you'll also receive: bandages for wounds, freedom, light, favor, defense, comfort, provision, beauty, joy, and praise!"

Sounds like everything we need.

If followers of Christ have all of that, then what is left to fix? The mess mind-set can't exist in the presence of Jesus.

Self-loathing feeds on insecurity like fire feeds on oxygen. But when we experience Christ's love, we become—for the first time—secure. We no longer provide self-loathing what it needs to survive in our minds. The "I'm stuck" feeling extinguishes like a flame under a jar when the love of Jesus surrounds us.

As passionate followers of Jesus, we don't continue to retain our issues. We can let them go, admitting they might just be excuses not to change. In the Bible, we meet a woman who has had an issue of blood, or constant hemorrhaging, for twelve years. Jesus makes His way through the city, and people fill the streets until the "whole crowd is pressing up against" Him. The woman with the issue of blood presses in with them. But then she "came up behind [Jesus] and touched the edge of his cloak, and immediately her bleeding stopped."[5] We need to ask ourselves: If we still have issues, have we really taken hold of Jesus? Because the Word says that when we do, our issues stop. At least, our *acceptance* of our issues stops. We no longer talk about them as if we own our issues. Or as if they own us.

So what do we do?

Instead of accepting her issue, this woman *pressed in.*

The apostle Paul had an issue too. Whatever it was, he "begged the Lord to take it away" three times (2 Cor. 7:8 NLT).

Instead of accepting his issue, the apostle Paul *pressed on*:

I don't mean to say that I have already achieved these things or that I have already reached perfection. But I press on to possess that perfection for which Christ Jesus first possessed me. No, dear brothers and sisters, I have not achieved it, but I focus on this one thing: Forgetting the past and looking forward to what lies ahead, I press on to reach the end of the race and receive the heavenly prize for which God, through Christ Jesus, is calling us.[6]

We don't need to be perfect, but we do need to be in pursuit. We can press in, press on, and take hold of Jesus for permanent healing and transformation. Our words are divinely empowered to achieve a specific outcome, and if we call ourselves messes who have issues, then that is what we will be. But calling ourselves healed and whole will usher us into a different ending. Also, now I know why the old way of trying to retool my heart never worked. The solution was so much simpler than I had dreamed. This occurred to me when I was reading a familiar chapter in Exodus, and the words almost leaped off the page and danced before my eyes in the dining room where I was drinking my morning coffee. Like light searing through the chaos, I saw a connection I had not seen before.

In that passage, Moses presents the Ten Commandments to the Israelites, speaking on behalf of God. He says,

> Build for me an *altar made of earth*, and offer your sacrifices to me. . . . If you use stones to build my altar, use only natural, uncut stones. Do not shape the stones with a tool, for that would make the altar unfit for holy use.[7]

The moment I read it, I thought of how we don't offer sacrifices on altars today. Instead, God asks us to be "a living sacrifice," offering our entire lives to Him.[8] Now we are *both* the altar *and* the sacrifice. God made humans from the dust of the ground. That means we are not only altars but *altars made of earth*, which is exactly what God was asking for in Exodus.

God does not change.[9] Jesus is "the same yesterday and today and forever."[10] He is "the one who is, who always was, and who is still to come."[11] Therefore, when we want God to remake us, we must look at how He made us in the first place. If we long for new life, we must look at how He brought life to Adam.

He breathed into him.

New life is only possible with the breath of Jesus in us: the Holy Spirit.

Jesus follows a distinct pattern when He makes us new. New creation is not sudden any more than Creation was sudden; there is a divine sequence. In fact, for many of the acts of the Creation "week," there is a distinct corresponding action displayed in the life of Jesus. The most stunning is the connection between the empowering breath of the Creator into Adam and the empowering breath of the Savior into His disciples. In the tender moments after His resurrection, the Author of Life wastes no time in sharing new life. His disciples are gathered in their grief to discuss what to do now that Jesus is crucified, when Jesus Himself suddenly walks through the door. Not through an open door, but *through a locked door*. He greets them in peace, and "then he [takes] a deep breath and [breathes] into them. 'Receive the Holy Spirit.'"[12]

This is how He gives new life.

The Creator formed chaos into what He called "good" by establishing a sequence that builds in beauty and complexity. He will transform our chaos into what is good by using the same divine sequence if we rely on the power of the Holy Spirit He has breathed into us:

- On Day One, He said, "Let there be light." And there was light. With re-creation, that is *Revelation*.
- On Day Two, He said, "Let there be a space called *sky*." And the waters divided. With re-creation, that is *Freedom*.
- On Day Three, He said, "Let there be order." And the waters flowed into position so that land could appear. With re-creation, that is *Purpose*. Then He said, "Let there be fruitfulness." The land burst forth with vegetation. With re-creation, that is *Productivity*.
- On Day Four, He said, "Let there be direction." And the sun and moon appeared in order to be signs to mark the seasons, days, and years. With re-creation, that is *Guidance*.
- On Day Five, He said, "Let there be life." And the seas teemed with animals that swim and the skies with animals that fly. With re-creation, that is *Community*.
- On Day Six, He said, "Let there be *more* life." And the land abounded with animals that were subject to us. With re-creation, that is *Authority*. Then He said, "Let them be made in My image." And human beings came to life,

divinely created to pass on God's DNA throughout all generations. With re-creation, that is *Legacy*.

- On Day Seven, He rested. With re-creation, that is *Renewal*.

The divine sequence of Creation reveals the divine sequence of new creation.

We, God's altars of earth, *began* when He created us from the ground. Ours are the real, dust-bound, uncut lives that He desires as a sacrifice. He doesn't want the ideal lives in our minds; He doesn't ask for improved lives that have been shaped by our self-help tools. We are His creation *and* we are His new creation. He was the One who *formed* us. And only through Him are we *transformed*. We will never be able to do it ourselves, not with any tool. Transformation is supernatural; it comes from the Holy Spirit alone.

Do you desire to change or completely start over? He wants us just as we are, simple altars of earth, so that His hands are the only ones shaping us.

Just as it was *in the Beginning*.

The First Day

In the beginning God created the heavens and the earth.
Now the earth was formless and empty, darkness was over
the surface of the deep, and the Spirit of God
was hovering over the waters. And God said,
"Let there be light," and there was light.
God saw that the light was good, and he separated
the light from the darkness. God called the light "day,"
and the darkness he called "night." And there was evening,
and there was morning—the first day.

—

GENESIS 1:1–5

Something is there in the darkness.

It is vacant, but something is there. It is called *earth*. This nebulous thing has substance but no meaning; it is formless. Its essence is disaster, complete chaos. It is shrouded in deep waters. Though the waters are deep, they are devoid of purpose. They cannot sustain life.

Someone is there in the darkness, looking upon the ruin.

"Before [Him] no god was formed, nor will there be one after [Him]."[1] He hovers over the lifeless deep, waiting to speak. He inhales. Then with a resonant breath He calls forth "each new generation from the beginning of time."[2]

"Let there be light!" He says.

At His word, brilliance rips through confusion, tearing turmoil in two. Layers of night peel away, blowing apart like ash. At His word, a gash of luminosity opens upon the curtain of disorder. From that instant and forevermore, there will be a limit to what darkness can do. Chaos will no longer have its way.

Jesus *is* the Light of the World.

On Day One, God answers darkness with Himself.

ONE

Let There Be Light

AS HARD AS IT IS to picture this bizarre theater of our origin, it is harder to imagine how it approached that point. What was there? In the seven-day Creation account, was God making the heavens and the earth out of substance He had already created previously, or was He creating substance from nothing for the first time?

Some details remain a mystery. The Bible gives us just enough information to establish our faith, but never so much as to obliterate us, which the full knowledge of eternity would certainly do. Whatever the substance was, it was chaos—either in catastrophic ruins or in embryonic beginnings. How events came to that point is irrelevant to our exploration. This is not that kind of book; I am not a theologian.

Neither will we discuss how events led to this point in your life (you can thank me later). This is not that kind of book; I am not a psychologist. We will focus singularly on moving forward from here, on our personal re-creation according to the divine sequence of Creation.

What is important for us to take away from the first paragraph in Genesis is a glimpse of God. In the first words of the Bible we see that He is positioned to make all things new. He is in the same position with us right now.

This is very good news. Because the disorder that existed before humanity reminds me of a different kind of disorder. Read the descriptions below and try not to wince.

> The LORD looks down from heaven
>   on all mankind
> to see if there are any who understand,
>   any who seek God.
> All have turned away, all have become corrupt;
>   there is no one who does good,
>   not even one.[3]

> For although they knew God, they neither glorified him as God nor gave thanks to him, but their thinking became futile and their foolish hearts were darkened. . . . They exchanged the truth about God for a lie, and worshiped and served created things rather than the Creator—who is forever praised.[4]

What does that sound like? To me, it sounds a lot like the world we are living in.

And it also sounds like darkness and chaos. These are descriptions of human beings trying to do things without God. This is the picture of what we create when we try to create something ourselves. Where a human life is concerned, a DIY project doesn't mean Do It Yourself. It means *Destroy It Yourself.*

> Cursed is the one who trusts in man,
>> who draws strength from mere flesh
>> and whose heart turns away from the LORD. . . .
> But blessed is the one who trusts in the LORD,
>> whose confidence is in him.[5]

Cursed is the one who trusts in man. Cursed! We simply can't remake ourselves. But God still hovers over ruined waters, waiting to speak.

When I read the first chapter of Genesis, my imagination takes a quick pan of the area, and I picture something like a ghost swan, gliding across a dark sea, its aerial glow brightening the tide. But it isn't a ghost, of course; it is the Spirit of God on the surface of the water.

God on the surface of the water.

God.

On the surface of the water.

My heart whispers to me that I have seen this image before, and suddenly a familiar scene fills my mind. There He is in Galilee, walking on water. This is no thin specter; it is Jesus, emboldened, hovering over the deep. He stands on tanned, sandaled feet.

> At about four o'clock in the morning, Jesus came toward them walking on the water. They were scared out of their wits. "A ghost!" they said, crying out in terror. But Jesus was quick to comfort them. "Courage, it's me. Don't be afraid."[6]

The disciples think Jesus is a ghost; they don't recognize Him as being alive. Notice the rich connection between this famous scene of water walking and the indiscernible opening of the Creation account. We talk about that New Testament miracle on the Sea of Galilee as if it were Jesus's *first* time to walk on water.

But maybe He had done it before.

Pay close attention to who was present at the Creation of the world:

> In the beginning the Word already existed.
> > The Word was with God,
> > and the Word was God.
> He existed in the beginning with God.
> God created everything through him,
> > and nothing was created except through him.
> The Word gave life to everything that was created,
> > and his life brought light to everyone.
> The light shines in the darkness,
> > and the darkness can never extinguish it.[7]

Jesus is the Word. He was not only there at the point of Creation, but as the Word, He is the One who did the speaking. Have you ever pictured that Jesus's voice said, "Let there be light"? Or did the events always play out in your mind as being from someone with a Santa Claus face and a Darth Vader voice? Or was it just a voice with no face? I used to think of it that way. But now I picture Jesus creating. It is no wonder that the disciples do not recognize Him walking on the waters in Genesis 1. Neither do most people recognize their Creator's voice today. The Bible says as much:

> The one who is the true light, who gives light to everyone,

was coming into the world. He came into the very world he created, but the world didn't recognize him.[8]

Jesus came into the very world *He created*.

Yes, Jesus was there—being Jesus, doing what Jesus does—on Day One. The Bible tells us that "Jesus Christ is the same yesterday and today and forever,"[9] so we have every reason to believe that what His disciples saw Him do in Israel was not just a sudden and temporary phase. Walking on water and speaking words of life are what Jesus *has been* doing, *is still* doing, and *will always* be doing. This truth opens our eyes to see something new about how to experience real and lasting life change.

In order to be re-created, we need the Creator to speak. The Creator is Jesus.

"I am the light of the world," Jesus says to the crowds who have gathered to hear Him teach.[10] We can imagine Him lost in thought after He says this, drifting for a moment in memory, going back to the instant when He had said, "Let there be light." Even then, He was summoning Himself, the Light of the World, to be our Savior in all ways.

When we study the method that Jesus uses to create, we learn how He re-creates as well. His voice is how He created, and without His voice, there is nothing. His voice is over the waters. His voice is over all.

> The voice of the LORD is over the waters;
> The God of glory thunders;
> The LORD is over many waters.
> The voice of the LORD is powerful;
> The voice of the LORD is full of majesty.[11]

Maybe you need re-creation today, and you want Jesus to speak into your heart. As we journey through the divine sequence, focus on listening to His voice rather than your own. Remember when I said DIY stands for Destroy It Yourself? We accomplish nothing when we take His voice out of the equation. If we try to conquer habits alone, we only end up looking at our problems and then looking at ourselves, and realizing it doesn't add up. That's what Peter did when Jesus called him.

> Jumping out of the boat, Peter walked on the water to Jesus. But when he looked down *at the waves churning beneath his feet*, he lost his nerve and started to sink.[12]

God says that He has put everything under our feet. So we think we should be able to stomp on addictions and appetites. We try to harness heavy desire with thought. We try to beat back compulsion with willpower.

Why isn't it working?

Everything may be under our feet, but let's be honest: a lot of times, when we glance down, the stuff under our feet is churning. If we rely only on our might while we're standing on the stormy waves of what we want, we sink. The waters beneath us are ruined. Those waters are dark and deep. Those waters are chaos. If we look down, we will go down.

Jesus wasn't kidding when He said, "Human effort accomplishes nothing."[13]

When He said "nothing," I think He meant . . . *nothing*.

But He also said, "If you follow me, you won't have to walk in darkness, because you will have the light that leads to life."[14]

Water-walking is not in our skill set, but it has always been in His. *Keep your eyes on Me*, Jesus reassures us as we place a timid foot on the sea, *and you will be able to see the next step to take. Don't look down now. Don't look down.*

It is not about our willpower. It is about His will and His power, so that is where we keep our attention. I love what the book of Hebrews tells us about keeping our eyes on Him.

> You made [humans] a little lower than the angels; you crowned them with glory and honor and put everything under their feet. In putting everything under them, God left nothing that is not subject to them. Yet at present we do not see everything subject to them. *But we do see Jesus.*[15]

In the very sentence that tells of our beginning, we learn of our identity. We are children of the Living God, and we are vested with godly authority and rights. All things in heaven and on earth answer to God, therefore all things must answer to us because we are made in His image.

I can hear you say, "Again . . . *why* isn't it working?"

This is the problem, as Hebrews explains it: everything is under our feet, but for now we do not see evidence of it. But we *do* see Jesus. And when we see Jesus, He brings light to the chaos. That light is called *revelation*.

What I am calling revelation, Dallas Willard calls *vision*. He writes, "The key, then, to loving God is to *see Jesus*, to hold him before the mind with as much fullness and clarity as possible."[16] Willard suggests that "seeing Jesus" is split into four critical aspects.

> First, we see his beauty, truth, and power while he lived among us as one human being among others. . . .
>
> Second, we see the way he went to execution as a common criminal among other criminals on our behalf. . . .

Third, we see the reality of Jesus risen, his actual existence now as a person who is present among his people. . . .

But fourth, we see the Jesus who is the master of the created universe and of human history. He is the one in ultimate control of all the atoms, particles, quarks, "strings," and so forth upon which the physical cosmos depends.

Human beings have long aspired to control the ultimate foundations of ordinary reality. We have made a little progress, and there remains an unwavering sense that this is the direction of our destiny. That is the theological meaning of the scientific and technological enterprise. It has always presented itself to "man on his own" as the instrument for solving human problems. But without a divine context it becomes idolatrous and veers wildly out of human control, threatening self-destruction.[17]

Simply put, first we open our eyes to see that Jesus *lived*. Second, that He *died*. Third, that He *lives again*. And fourth, that this living Jesus is *Creator and Master* of all things. We are not supposed to solve problems on our own; we are to submit every concern to the One who made it all . . . and can make it all new.

In the book of Revelation we witness Jesus sitting on a throne and saying, "'I am making everything new!' Then he says, '*Write this down*, for these words are trustworthy and true.'"[18]

The Creator and Master is making all things new, including *you*. How He makes things new, as we have said, is with His voice. And because we are made in His image, we must join Him in what He does. Therefore, for each of the nine creative acts of Creation/re-creation, we are going to *put in writing and then repeat out loud* a particular scripture. That is our strategy. The series of declarations we will make are based on complete passages pulled directly from the Bible. They are not just positive statements that I have written myself. In some cases, I have changed pronouns (such as "you" to "I") in order to make the scripture apply personally.

On Day One, the Creator spoke into chaos, "Let there be light." Now it's your turn to say it to yourself. I am about to give you the first declaration to write down in a journal or notebook. You are going to call out revelation for yourself, so write your name in the appropriate blank. Then go to a mirror, look yourself in the eye, and begin reading the declaration out loud to yourself. Of course, you will have to look down to read the page, but be sure to look up every few sentences and make eye contact with yourself. When people are serious about something—when they are making vows, contracts, or agreements—they look one another in the eye. You are going to look yourself in the eye because you are getting serious with yourself today. It is time to make an agreement with yourself about who God says you are, even if you do not see evidence of it right now. If it feels too weird or awkward to look yourself in the eye as you read this declaration, then your first problem is revealing itself.

You *must* be able to speak God's words to yourself in order to be re-created. No wonder it hasn't been happening.

It is not strange to look yourself in the eye; it is healthy. In fact, it is absolutely vital that you keep trying to look yourself in the eye and read God's Word over yourself every day until you can do it easily. Don't give up! It took me six months to become comfortable looking into a mirror and reading God's Word aloud over myself.

By the way, do not skip writing down His words, because that is what He tells us to do in the verse above. Put it in writing! Do not take a shortcut and read silently either. Thinking these words is not the same thing. Remember, Jesus did not *think* Creation into being. He *spoke* it into being.

Let There Be Revelation
(from Ephesians 1:17-23)

I, _____, keep asking that the God of our Lord Jesus Christ, the glorious Father, may give me the Spirit of wisdom and revelation, so that I may know Him better. I pray that the eyes of my heart may be enlightened in order that I may know the hope to which He has called me, the riches of His glorious inheritance in His holy people, and His incomparably great power for us who believe. That power is the same as the mighty strength He exerted when He raised Christ from the dead and seated Him at His right hand in the heavenly realms, far above all rule and authority, power and dominion, and every name that is invoked, not only in the present age but also in the one to come. And God placed all things under His feet and appointed Him to be head over everything for the church, which is His body, the fullness of Him who fills everything in every way.

After you have completed your first task, congratulations are in order! Begin looking for ways that God gives you revelation in the coming days or weeks.

This may be new to you, and you may wonder how you are supposed to discern God's voice. It may be according to your learning style. When I taught English in public schools, I became acquainted with three learning styles that categorize most students. Good teachers know they can't present a new concept or information toward only one learning style because other students might miss it. Within the church, I can see that God does the same thing, to some extent.

Believers who are auditory learners tend to learn by hearing. God may communicate with you by speaking through another Christian. He may use the words of a song that comes on the radio or one that comes to mind and gets stuck in your head. He may let you "hear" a word or sentence in your heart. When this has happened to me, it wasn't as if I heard an audible voice in the room; I "heard" it in my heart. Except they were thoughts I had never thought before and were contrary to my first instinct or desire. Yes, sometimes God's voice "sounds" like your own inner voice, but He won't say what you would say. That's the difference.

The other day a friend asked me, "While I was at the grocery store, I noticed the woman in front of me was very tired and worn out. Suddenly I thought I'd like to buy all of her groceries. Was that me or was that God? I didn't do it because it seemed like it was just me. It sounded like my voice." With this example, it is pretty clear. God's were the thoughts that motivated her to give. Hers were the thoughts that decided not to do it.

Look, it is not human instinct to give. An infant doesn't give. It only knows how to take. A toddler doesn't know how to be unselfish. Our human flesh is naturally wired that way. Believe me, you do not naturally want to spend $100 on someone else's groceries. If you think an unselfish thought, that is God within you, supernaturally motivating you.

Believers who are visual learners tend to learn by seeing. God may communicate with you by drawing your attention to a billboard or an image in a magazine. He may bring you new understanding as you observe a scene around you. He may send you a dream, memory, or vision.

When I have experienced a vision, it wasn't like being in a

trance; it was like what happens when I can vividly picture a memory in my mind. I'm sure this has happened to you before. You can be driving down the street and see a house that reminds you of a childhood friend, and suddenly you can picture everything about playing in that friend's backyard. You can "see" the memory in your mind even while you are still driving and still seeing what is before your eyes. Except you will know it is a vision and not a memory because you have never seen it before.

And about dreams, how can we know that a dream is a significant dream from God and not just an average dream on a restless night? We ask Him. He will be faithful to let us know eventually. But usually I know immediately upon waking that the dream is meaningful because I sense the Holy Spirit teaching me something important through the dream.

Believers who are kinesthetic learners tend to learn by doing. God may communicate with you by letting you have a strong feeling about the next step you should take. He may allow you to feel nauseated by something you should avoid or feel a sense of urgency or peace about something you should pursue. You might even experience a bodily sensation, such as tingling in your fingers or hands.

When I have experienced something like this, it could be described as an intuitive "knowing" in my chest or gut that I couldn't really explain. You might find yourself explaining it to friends by saying, "I have prayed about this and read what the Bible says about it, and I just *know* this is what I need to do."

Whether you receive auditory, visual, or kinesthetic revelation, measure it against Scripture. God will never communicate something that is contrary to His Word. The important thing is to stay aware. Keep reading your written declaration of revelation over yourself until your eyes are opened to the detailed and unique things in your life that need to change. Only the Holy Spirit can minister to your life *specifically*. No two readers' answers and actions will be entirely the same. Every journey will be different. But my guess is that all of ours will require some action. You will have to *move* in some way. By inviting the Word of God into your life, you have unlocked the prison door. But just because the prison door has been unlocked doesn't mean that you are free yet. Be ready to step out when He says step out.

A friend of mine has now gone to be with the Lord. In her fifty years on earth, she suffered many tragedies, including being captured and imprisoned in her small country on the continent of Africa. While in confinement, she and the other women endured unspeakable brutality.

Then, after another night of terrifying violence, the guards left the women's quarters . . . but this time they accidentally left the door unlocked.

My friend waited until the guards were so drunk that they fell asleep, then she whispered to her fellow captives, "We leave tonight! The door is unlocked! Come with me!"

She was stunned when some of them stared at her, motionless.

"What will we eat?" they asked with broken and blank faces. "What will we drink? Where will we hide?"

"Come! We'll find bread! We'll find water. We'll find covering! Just come!"

She moved toward the open door, but they hesitated. She could not wait for them to decide. With very little time left, she ran into the night, leaving most of the women behind.

Who are we to be amazed at this? As unthinkable as it is, we do it every day. Sometimes it is easier to stay with what we know, even if what we know is bondage. If only those women had realized there would have been a good chance of survival if they had run into the dark together.

The plans we have made for our lives may seem safe, but some of them are prisons. We need God's plan instead of our own. Self-sufficiency and self-protection will keep us locked away from the God who loves us and longs to fulfill our needs Himself. Any comfort made on our own is a cell. The very thing we are holding on to could be holding us back. God wants us to move as Jesus did—in the freedom of total trust in His Father.

We have been strong so long; we have been holding on. But we may have been holding on to iron bars. Open your calloused hands with me. It is time to flee from the cell of self.

Just come. We leave tonight. God has unlocked the door, and He promises this: We will find Bread. We will find Water. We will find Covering. His name is Jesus.

Let's move from the darkness into the Light.

TWO

Revelation

AT NINE O'CLOCK in the evening, I was not expecting a knock at the door.

"Have you seen Carrie?" a neighbor asked. "Her mother is worried and has called the police. The two of them had a small disagreement about cleaning her room tonight, and then Carrie left on her bike an hour ago. Her mother has to stay home with the other children, and her father is out of town. He is on his way home right now so I'm going door-to-door to check if anyone has seen her."

There was reason for concern about finding the twelve-year-old. Several abduction attempts had been reported in our hometown news that summer. And though I'd always waved at Carrie as she rode her bike throughout the neighborhood, I'd never seen her out too late. Now there were only a few minutes of mid-August twilight left.

Before my friend and I finished speaking, it was dark.

Immediately, a crew of neighbors poured into the streets, some walking, some driving. Flashlight beams shone from tree branches to bushes. Everyone was calling her name. A handful of cops strategically moved into the area, patrolling two local parks and the school around the corner. Some stationed their vehicles at entrances to the neighborhood and at Carrie's house.

Later that night, she came home. She had ridden her bike to a distant park that she'd only been driven to before. To get there, she'd had to cross a busy six-lane boulevard on which cars routinely travel fifty miles per hour or more. At the park, she'd sat by herself for about forty-five minutes, thinking about the argument and hoping her mother would feel sorry enough to change her mind about the household chores. She'd felt confident about her decision to run out on her mother until about 9:00 p.m. . . . when the light ran out on her.

Carrie's young bravado left at the same time. What had seemed like a good idea suddenly proved to be a mistake. She had not anticipated being alone in the park at night. She jumped anxiously when streetlamps sputtered and buzzed above her. Long shadows stretched from the trees, bending back and forth as the wind moaned through the playground equipment. She spun around when she heard footsteps echo from the adjacent parking lot. She turned again when chimes sounded from a house behind her. Soon she was consumed with fear. *What am I doing here?* she thought.

The darkness doubled the danger.

The darkness put things into perspective.

The darkness drove her home.

Getting on her bike, she headed back to her house, where her mother and her father were waiting for her. As soon as she arrived, she jumped off her bike and ran into the beam of the front-porch light.

And into her father's embrace.

In another ten minutes, the neighbors on the search got the two-word text we were praying for: "She's home."

Every one of us knows what it is like to be Carrie, to look around and feel the chill of falling darkness. No matter how we came into our situations—whether because of our own decisions or someone else's or the simple fact that life is unexpected—there is only one thing to do when we find ourselves there: head home.

Our Father's embrace awaits us.

The lovely father portrait in Jesus's parable of the lost son is what we might picture here. You are probably familiar with this account of a father who had two sons. The youngest asks for his inheritance and leaves home for good, only to waste every penny and find himself working in a pigpen, hungry enough to consider eating what the pigs are eating. *What am I doing here?* he thinks. There in the pen he suddenly realizes that he would rather go back to his father and "eat crow" than stay in the far country and eat pig slop. He begins the homeward journey, rehearsing his apology with every step he takes.

Many grace-laced sermons have helped us imagine the father's elation when he saw his son's silhouette limping on the horizon. Instantly, his heart was "filled with love and compassion, he ran to his son, embraced him, and kissed him."[19] Their reunion was astonishing. The son must have thought it was a miracle that he received a hero's welcome. But the miraculous part of the story, the part that captivates me, is a few verses earlier and is woefully brief at seven words:

"When he finally came to his senses . . ."[20]

Tell me more! What made the lost son want to go home? Did he flash back to a happy scene from his childhood? Did the words of his father's loving good-bye come echoing back to him? Did he see something, hear something, taste something that made him miss the security of the old days? Whatever it was, he suddenly faced the facts. He stopped blaming his father for his own discontentment. He stopped regretting the choice he had miserably wasted.

He put down the blame and regret and headed back home.

Why did the lost son come to his senses?

It might have been the same thing that made Carrie put down her blame and regret.

Things got dark.

If you deeply desire to begin again, it may be because you recently have emerged from a season of chaos, cold, or darkness. You have survived and you are ready—oh, so *ready!*—for beauty, warmth, and the brightness of spring. In your haste to walk out of winter, however, don't forget to double-check your cargo. What are you carrying? God designed our hearts to be fertile ground so whatever seeds you bring with you will grow. There are two things you do not want to take when you leave the pigpens of the past: blame and regret.

They are the dangers of yesterday. They have no business in today.

To blame is to live in a state of constant accusation toward others. It is easy to blame someone for what is behind us. We blame Satan for this or that. We blame our bosses, our spouses, our parents, our children. We even blame God.

Blame toward others may be a thought that *enters*, but it cannot be a thought that we *entertain*.

Blame toward ourselves goes by a different name: regret. To regret is to live in a state of constant mourning over something we did or did not do. It is rehearsing again and again the same unalterable scenario, only to experience the grief all over again.

Regretting is re-grieving.

Both blame and regret are rooted in fear. Anything that grows out of fear will bring poisonous fruit, filled with spreading seeds. And fear-based fruit will always reproduce. It will become tree after tree after terrified tree that we continue to tend in our minds. We can get stuck blaming and regretting for years. For *years*. Planting destructive thoughts of blame or regret will lead to personal paralysis. Both will turn our attention in the wrong direction. Instead of letting us look toward the future, blame and regret keep us looking toward the past. We cannot get out of the miserable orchard, even when its harvest is making us sick.

Refusing to blame or regret will require raw trust. Some of the events in the pigpens of the past are so painful that they cannot be explained without bringing questions about God. What did He have to do with it? Why didn't He do anything? We have a choice whether we will let our understanding of God inform our understanding of our circumstances, or the other way around. If we believe God is taking good care of us even when things are uncomfortable or don't go our way, then He will sustain us with supernatural, incomprehensible peace. This peace in the present results in raw trust for the future. Raw trust prepares a rare path of spiritual progress, and "some extraordinary thing happens to a man who holds on to the love of God when the odds are against God's character."[21]

Theologian Alan Redpath writes of God's sovereignty in allowing difficulty in our lives,

There is nothing—no circumstance, no trouble, no testing—that can ever touch me until, first of all, it has gone past God and past Christ right through to me. If it has come that far, it has come with a great purpose, which I may not understand at the moment. But as I refuse to become panicky, as I lift up my eyes to Him and accept it as coming from the throne of God for some great purpose of blessing to my own heart, no sorrow will ever disturb me, no trial will ever disarm me, no circumstance will cause me to fret—for I shall rest in the joy of what my Lord is![22]

If things have been dark in your recent or distant past, then you must exchange blame and regret for trust. Every trial comes with a great purpose. But what is that purpose? Why does God do what He does? Why does He allow uncomfortable—even painful—things to happen to His children?

He allows darkness "so that [people] should seek the Lord, in the hope that they might grope for Him and find Him, though He is not far from each one of us."[23] In other words, He allows darkness so that we will come to our senses and seek the Light.

Perhaps only when we have been blinded and cannot sense the future beyond our ache will we reach out with open arms and feeble fingers to feel for Him. And when we do, He is glorified. We are not on this earth for our own benefit. We exist to glorify God. That is our purpose. Everything God does is for His glory. He permits painful periods because nothing glorifies Him more than the life of a faith-battered believer who may feel like *turning away* from God, but keeps *turning to* Him instead. All of heaven applauds that kind of surrender.

You can't live in the past or the future. When we invite the Creator to make us new, we must put down any blame and regret we carry and go back, not back to the past, but back to our Father.

He is the One who brings us to our senses.

"How foolish can you be?" Paul writes. "After starting your

new lives in the Spirit, why are you now trying to become perfect by your own human effort?"[24]

I can see Jesus shaking His head from heaven, thinking, *I already told them "human effort accomplishes nothing."*[25]

Go back to the Beginning. Go back to the Spirit who hovered over the waters. You can't create a new life on your own. Only the Author of Life can do that.

That is why we must put down blame and regret. It is hard to submit to the Spirit when our arms are loaded with chaotic questions (*What does it all mean? Why did it have to happen this way? Have I wasted too much time? Where did I go wrong? Is there any hope left? Where do I begin?*). Submitting means dropping our demands for an explanation of the past in favor of the raw trust that glorifies and richly honors God in the present.

Raw trust is submission. Submission means letting go of blame and regret—and some questions—forever, purposefully closing the door to those thoughts whenever they nose back in. Submission means leaning on God with our whole heart and refusing to depend on our own understanding.[26] Submission means obeying, no matter what He asks.

Submission means dying to ourselves.

Jesus promises that this surrender-death gives way to new life. It starts an unstoppable process. He makes an analogy, connecting the human heart to the rest of creation, saying that "unless a kernel of wheat is planted in the soil and dies, it remains alone. But its death will produce many new kernels—a plentiful harvest of new lives."[27]

Wheat is buried in soil, but we are buried somewhere else when we die to ourselves. Colossians 3:3 tells us where: "For you died to this life, and your real life is hidden with Christ in God" (NLT).

What it means to be hidden, or buried, in Christ is to stop living for our agenda, taking on His life as our own. When Christ died, the Father didn't leave Him in the tomb. He won't leave us buried either. Just as resurrection surely followed Jesus's death, revelation will surely follow our death to self.

You can be assured that "if the Spirit of him who raised Jesus from the dead is living in you, he who raised Christ from the dead will also give life to *your mortal bodies* because of his Spirit who lives in you."[28] This refers to every aspect of our lives in the here and now.

You don't have to wait until heaven to embrace the resurrected life, as you may have thought. God says, "You're a hard-headed bunch and hard to help. I'm ready to help you right now. Deliverance is not a long-range plan. Salvation isn't on hold."[29] This verse sounds even more urgent with the exclamation point that is in this translation: "I am ready to set things right, not in the distant future, but *right now*!"[30]

He's ready. Are we?

It is time to come to your senses, to let God illuminate the way you have been living versus the way to live from now on, as a new creation in the Spirit. Keep reading Scripture over yourself daily. Keep listening for God's word of revelation about your situation. You and I cannot see in the dark on our own.

Chances are, the things we tend to think about from our pasts are not the things that He is wanting to address. The memories we dwell on through blame and regret are probably only decoys the enemy has set up in an attempt to keep our eyes off of the real areas that need a touch from God. As you ask for revelation, let the Holy Spirit lead your thoughts, bringing His focal points from your past and present to your attention.

It seems too good to be true that Jesus could speak and there would be instantaneous and inextinguishable light in the original darkness. Yet, it happened. Do we dare believe that Jesus could speak and there would be instantaneous and inextinguishable light in our hearts as well? It rings like a promise, and we are assured that "no matter how many promises God has made, they are 'Yes' in Christ."[31]

I heard that verse about "yes and amen" more than a thousand times before I understood it. It wasn't until the thousand and first time that I realized I had been repeating it incorrectly. I had misquoted it as saying all God's promises are yes and amen in Christ. But the Word says only the "Yes" is in Christ. Jesus speaks and the impossible becomes possible.

The "Amen" is spoken by *us*.

The rest of the verse and the ones following really read: "And so through him the 'Amen' *is spoken by us* to the glory of God. Now it is God who makes both us and you stand firm in Christ. He anointed us, set his seal of ownership on us, and put his Spirit in our hearts as a deposit, guaranteeing what is to come."[32]

By the Spirit in us as a deposit guaranteeing what is to come, we say "Amen" to every creative word Christ speaks! I tremble at the privilege. We must agree with Him. That agreement must be spoken.

The message of this book is not new. The message of this book is not varied. The message of this book is not a secret, and you don't have to wait for it. Here it is: "If you declare with your mouth, 'Jesus is Lord,' and believe in your heart that God raised him from the dead, you will be saved. For it is with your heart that you believe and are justified, and it is *with your mouth* that you profess your faith and are saved."[33] This miraculous process applies, not only once, but continually. By believing in our hearts and declaring with our mouths, we are saved from hell. With the same process, won't we also be saved from habits?

Every sentence in these pages hinges on the assumption that you already have given your life to Christ. If you have not made the decision to place your life in submission to Jesus, the Creator of the universe, then keep reading. Hopefully, by the last page, you will have become acquainted with some new truths. And you will surrender yourself to Him for the first time.

If you already are a Christian—a term that means "little Christ"—then you can expect Christ to live in and through you. I'll show you many of the ways He does that, so keep reading. Hopefully, by the last page, you will become reacquainted with some old truths. And you will surrender yourself to Him again.

The Message translation paraphrases the foundational scripture of this book to perfection: "The word that saves is right here, as near as the tongue in your mouth, as close as the heart in your chest." Furthermore, we read:

> It's the word of faith that welcomes God to go to work and set things right for us. This is the core of our preaching. Say the welcoming word to God—"Jesus is my Master"— embracing, body and soul, God's work of doing in us what he did in raising Jesus from the dead. That's it. You're not "doing" anything; you're simply calling out to God, trusting him to do it for you. That's salvation. With your whole being you embrace God setting things right, and *then you say it, right out loud*: "God has set everything right between him and me!"[34]

"I am the light of the world," Jesus says.

"Amen!" we say out loud.

"So let there be light," Jesus says.

"Amen!" we say out loud.

And with that confession, we finally invite Him into our darkened chaos. Then the Spirit—the guarantee living inside us and the seal of God's ownership on our lives—has our permission to bring us the light we've longed for, because we are finally using our words to agree with the One who is Light.

Light is where new life begins.

The Second Day

Then God said, "Let there be a space between the waters,
to separate the waters of the heavens from
the waters of the earth." And that is what happened.
God made this space to separate the waters of the earth
from the waters of the heavens. God called the space "sky."
And evening passed and morning came,
marking the second day.

—

GENESIS 1:6–8 NLT

Reaching out across the light He has just created, Jesus dips His hand into the waters. They are no longer dark. When the light came, they lost their murky mystery. Now they are exposed and at His disposal. He can move them at His will.

The same Creator who easily walks on water can just as easily divide water. Hundreds of years later, He will part the Red Sea so that Moses and the Israelites can walk across on dry ground. That event will only be an echo of what is about to happen.

With unimaginable strength, He pushes down the *waters of earth*: those shapeless masses of hydrogen and oxygen, moving in fluid obedience to His desire. Later, the waters of earth will become oceans, lakes, rivers, ice caps, and hidden groundwater pulsing in subterranean arteries. For now, they pool in a translucent plateau, still empty of life and waiting for an assignment.

Then His muscular hands slide under the *waters of heaven*: the armory of irrigation that He will reserve for discipline and the bounty He will store for blessing. Later, the waters of heaven will become rain, dew, clouds, snow, and hail. For now, they hang where He has lifted them, still empty of energy and waiting for an assignment.

"Let there be a space," He says.

On Day Two, God divides the waters to make room for the sky.

THREE

Let There Be a Space

WE KNOW THE WATERS of earth. We have not seen the waters of heaven, but we experience the evidence of them every day. They are kept somewhere beyond our conception. The Bible attests to this in various places, including the conversation between God and Job, during which God poetically reminds humanity of His sovereignty:

> Have you ever traveled to where snow is made,
>   seen the vault where hail is stockpiled,
> The arsenals of hail and snow that I keep in readiness
>   for times of trouble and battle and war? . . .
> Who do you suppose carves canyons
>   for the downpours of rain, and charts
>   the route of thunderstorms
> That bring water to unvisited fields,
>   deserts no one ever lays eyes on,
> Drenching the useless wastelands
>   so they're carpeted with wildflowers and grass?

And who do you think is the father of rain and dew,
    the mother of ice and frost?
You don't for a minute imagine
    these marvels of weather just happen, do you?[1]

The waters of the heavens are at the Creator's command, and one of His commands is that they praise Him.

Praise him, you highest heavens
    and you waters above the skies.
Let them praise the name of the LORD,
    for at his command they were created,
and he established them for ever and ever.[2]

Incidentally, if water is commanded to praise Him, then it should be obvious that we who are comprised of more than sixty percent water are commanded to praise Him as well.[3]

Pay attention to what God did on the Second Day, which was not exactly creating something out of nothing. It was separating the things He had already made.

And there was a space.

What God called *sky* is the atmosphere of earth, the expanse that extends from the air around our feet out into the edge of the universe, ranging from a thickness of air that humans can breathe to a thinness we cannot. Though Earth's atmosphere seems weightless to us, scientists report that it consists of a great deal of weight and exerts pressure, enough to press down the seas. Without the compression of the earth's atmosphere and gravity to hold it in place, the Pacific Ocean would float like dollops of Tang inside the space shuttle. Without the compression of the earth's atmosphere and gravity to hold *us* in place, we would drift to our schools and workplaces like astronauts every morning. Evolutionists cannot make sense of the origin of this atmospheric sky space.

"It is thought that the current atmosphere resulted from a gradual release of gases both from the planet's interior and from the metabolic activities of life-forms," they guess.[4] But Earth did not emit its own atmosphere, no. Our planet and the life-forms thereon did not exist prior to the gaseous envelope that would cradle them both. God created a fantastic aerosol hammock *before* He hung the earth within it. This firmament is "in itself no thing, but only room for things."[5]

Room for things.

We are now at the second phase of the divine sequence. It is critical to submit to the arrangement of Creation events if we desire to be re-created. Sometimes I am tempted to dismiss this progression as I seek new life. I want to tend the land and taste the fruit right away. But humanity's genesis develops logically in the Creation account, and it can be viewed as a manual for humanity's regeneration, to be sure. First, we began with revelation, as we invite the Creator to shine light on the chaos in our lives. He illuminates what we need to change.

Next comes freedom, as we cooperate with the Creator to create space in our lives. Before there are new things, there must be room for new things.

What is the "atmosphere" or "space" of our lives, though? The space God established on the Second Day of Creation is understood as both the division and the link, the connective tissue between the waters of earth (which are seen) and the waters of heaven (which are unseen but currently existing). The space God establishes during the second step of re-creation can also be understood as a division and a link, the connective tissue between our life on earth (which is seen) and our life in heaven (which is unseen but currently existing). We read how this division and connection of waters was accomplished with *just a word* in the beginning, but wonder how this can be completed in our lives now.

Can it still be done with just a word?

Let's walk through it carefully:

God is the One who divided the waters at Creation. And everything the Creator God did was finished through, not just *a* word, but *the* Word. And in case there was any question about who the Word was, John explains,

> So the Word became human and made his home among us. He was full of unfailing love and faithfulness. And we have seen his glory, the glory of the Father's one and only Son.[6]

The Word is Jesus. The division of the waters was made through Him. And the division of ourselves is also made through Him. Yes, the division of ourselves can be accomplished with the Word. We read in Hebrews that "the word of God is alive and active. Sharper than any double-edged sword, it penetrates even to *dividing soul and spirit*, joints and marrow; it judges the thoughts and attitudes of the heart."[7]

The division of soul and spirit is something I did not understand—or even consider, really—for most of my life. I pictured myself with a bifold essence. I had a body and I had a soul or spirit. The soul and spirit were the same thing to me, the stuff of my interior life. I thought I was made up of the interior and exterior alone. When I believed this way, it left me with diminished power.

The best way to illustrate this would be to analyze a long battle

I had with the destructive emotion of jealousy. Jealousy used to be a critical place in my life that needed re-creation. For many years, I felt overwhelming waves of jealousy surrounding certain areas. An easy one to dissect here would be the area of my career.

Teaching is the call and assignment I have received from the Lord. For ten years, I taught English in public schools, but before that decade on campuses, I taught as a missionary school teacher in Asia and in Bible classes at church. In the time since I left the classroom, I have continued to teach through writing books and speaking at various conferences. I can safely assume that my work in the Kingdom of God will always reflect some aspect of my teaching task, which He has continually prepared me to do.[8]

When God calls us to a particular work, He uniquely equips and empowers us to complete that work. He prepares both us and the assignment ahead of time. With that knowledge, there should not be any reason to measure ourselves against other Christians. Comparison is a clashing of tasks, of one person's life against another's. God never asked that we all be the same. The Kingdom is a symphony. God doesn't design us to live from the exact series of musical notes. Neither does He want us to operate in comparison with one another. That is living in cacophony, as if every musician in the orchestra were playing a separate composition. We play from the same piece—the gospel of Jesus Christ—but God designs for us different skills and different projects within the music because He desires that the signature sound of His people be *harmony*. Harmony is rich and complex. You can't compare one line with another. All of the parts are important, and the composer's intention would not be fulfilled if any were missing.

To an extent, I understood this, but again and again, I would stop playing my part in order to peer around at other people in the orchestra. Not at *everybody*, mind you, but at other women who were playing the same instrument—women near my age who had been equipped to teach through writing and speaking. I compared myself to them, and then I would feel incompetent and frustrated, thinking I was behind everyone else. I wanted to be where they were. During this time, I thought jealousy was part of my personality. I perceived it as the impassioned response of a driven person. I thought jealousy bred competition, and competition fueled improvement. *If someone in your section is playing better*, I reasoned, *then rehearse more*. Work harder *and* smarter; it seemed like the right thing for a focused teacher to do. Jealousy didn't seem all that bad; it kept me ambitious.

God does not need to use jealousy as a motivational tool, though. In fact, He cautions against it. He more than cautions, He commands. When He authored the Ten Commandments, the final command listed was "You shall not covet."[9] I knew that, of course, but I parsed the definition, thinking that coveting was wanting someone *not* to have something. Jealousy seemed different from coveting to me, not as dangerous. I thought I wasn't coveting because I wasn't wanting to take anything *away* from anyone. I was just wanting to have it too.

But any form of desire that is not surrendered to God and to His will and timing is harmful. As I look at the Ten Commandments, covetousness, or *wanting what you do not have*, seems to be the original seed of most of the commands. "You shall not commit adultery" refers to the desire for another spouse. "You shall not steal" refers to the desire for other possessions. "Remember the Sabbath day by keeping it holy" refers to the desire for another day to earn. "You shall have no other gods before me" refers to the desire for another god.[10]

I didn't have victory in the area of coveting until I got real about it, called it what it was, and stopped lying to myself. If we lie to ourselves, to the world, and to God by calling sin pretty names, then we will never experience freedom. It's silly to cover sin with vocabulary. Any sin that we try to cover ourselves is one that cannot be covered by God. King David wrote beautifully of the freedom that comes through giving up inner deceit and aligning with Truth:

Blessed is the one
    whose transgressions are forgiven,
    whose sins are covered.
Blessed is the one
    whose sin the LORD does not count against them
    and in whose spirit is no deceit.

When I kept silent,
    my bones wasted away
    through my groaning all day long.
For day and night
    your hand was heavy on me;
my strength was sapped
    as in the heat of summer.

Then I acknowledged my sin to you
    and did not cover up my iniquity.
I said, "I will confess
    my transgressions to the LORD."
And you forgave
    the guilt of my sin.[11]

The Message puts it this way:

Then I let it all out;
I said, "I'll make a clean breast of my failures to GOD."
Suddenly the pressure was gone—
my guilt dissolved,
my sin disappeared.[12]

In the same way, I acknowledged and confessed that I was coveting, and miraculously, the pressure inside me was gone.

God did not design my personality with an inclination toward jealousy. His Word says He does not give "a craving for physical pleasure, a craving for everything we see, and pride in our achievements and possessions. These are not from the Father, but are from this world."[13] The Lord didn't want me to treat envy as a familiar pet who has the run of the house. He wanted me to keep it outside the door, to master it. But I didn't know how to do that. Beating jealousy seemed to come down to willpower. And if I couldn't even quit superficial habits like nail biting, then how was I supposed to halt a deep-seated emotion as strong as jealousy? I couldn't. I pouted and sulked, feeling like a failure and out of options. I am not the first person jealousy has affected.

Cain couldn't conquer it either.

In the book of Genesis, Cain felt the heart-crushing envy of his brother, Abel. "Why are you so angry?" the Lord asked him. "Why do you look so dejected? You will be accepted if you do what is right. But if you refuse to do what is right, then watch out! Sin is crouching at the door, eager to control you. But you must subdue it and be its master."[14]

Cain didn't listen. He heard jealousy's whimper on the back step, begging to come in.

How much harm could it do? Cain might have thought. He turned the handle. Honestly, sometimes negative emotions feel a little comforting, which is why we decide to let them visit for a while. Somehow staying angry makes us feel better. It makes us feel like something is being done.

All Cain did was open the door. He entertained envy for one day. *One.* What looked to him as harmless as a puppy was a wolverine that would tear him to shreds. By nightfall, he couldn't believe what he had done: his brother was dead, and the blood was on *his* hands.

As I write this, I am crying for Cain. I have never done that before. But I also have never put my life parallel to his. I have so much in common with Cain. Jealousy is my great temptation. It has been easy for me to think it is a lesser evil. I have opened the door and entertained envy many times. But we see in Cain's life the same original seed we saw with the other commandments I mentioned. "Do not murder," God warned. For Cain, what ended with murder began with covetousness. There but for the grace of God go I.

The analogy of the puppy and the wolverine keeps coming back to me. Wolverines are cute and appear cuddly, but if you reach out to pet one, you could lose an arm. Even their scientific name, *Gulo*, is deceptive.

Gulo. It could be a happy clown's name.

Gulo! It sounds like something an Italian street vendor would say as he waves a cone of gelato in your direction.

Well, actually, that last one might work.

Gulo is Latin for glutton. The wolverine is the glutton of gluttons. Its eyes are bigger than its stomach. A wolverine is the size of an average dog, weighing anywhere from twenty-two to seventy pounds. Its ferocious jaws and knife-like claws can take down animals twenty times its size. Its main prey are caribou and moose, which weigh between six hundred and fifteen hundred pounds. So if you spot a wolverine on your hiking trip in Canada, don't get ambitious and think you can fend it off with a stick. To a wolverine, a two-hundred-pound human would just be the appetizer.

I can't think of a picture more fitting for jealousy. Jealousy is a wolverine. It is the glutton of gluttons.

No matter how much we see, we are never satisfied. No matter how much we hear, we are not content.[15]

Just as Death and Destruction are never satisfied, so human desire is never satisfied.[16]

Whoever loves money never has enough; whoever loves wealth is never satisfied with their income.[17]

Jealousy is the carnivore at my door. You have your own sins, crouching close, whimpering for entrance. But God told Cain that he didn't have to open the door, that he could master it. It has to be true for us too. There has to be something we can do.

"The temptations in your life are no different from what others experience," Paul tells us. "And God is faithful. He will not allow the temptation to be more than you can stand. When you are tempted, he will show you a way out so that you can endure."[18]

Can't see a way out? It doesn't mean it isn't there. Moses looked out over the Red Sea and did not see a way out of Egypt either. But God's "road led through the sea, [his] pathway through the mighty waters—a pathway no one knew was there!"[19] My prayer for you is that He will show you a way out of temptation that you never knew was there.

A way out. That is where a right understanding of the division of soul and spirit comes in. It is actually possible to shed the useless rags of the soul. We can choose to dress in the divine garments of the Spirit. The next verses we will put in writing and read aloud over our lives have to do with a separation between who we were and who we are becoming.

Let There Be Freedom
(from Colossians 3:1-15 NLT)

Since I, _____, have been raised to new life with Christ, I will set my sights on the realities of heaven, where Christ sits in the place of honor at God's right hand. Lord, help me think about the things of heaven, not the things of earth. For I have died to this life, and my real life is hidden with Christ in God. And when Christ, who is my life, is revealed to the whole world, I will share in all His glory.

So, Lord, help me put to death the sinful, earthly things lurking within me. I will have nothing to do with sexual immorality, impurity, lust, and evil desires. I will not be greedy, for a greedy person is an idolater, worshiping the things of this world. . . . I used to do these things when my life was still part of this world. But now is the time to get rid of anger, rage, malicious behavior, slander, and dirty language. I will not lie to others, for I have stripped off my old sinful nature and all its wicked deeds. I will put on my new nature, and be renewed as I learn to know my Creator and become like Him. In this new life, it doesn't matter if I am a Jew or a Gentile, circumcised or uncircumcised, barbaric, uncivilized, slave, or free. Christ is all that matters, and He lives in all of us.

Since God chose me to be one of the holy people He loves, I must clothe myself with tenderhearted mercy, kindness, humility, gentleness, and patience. I will make allowances for others' faults, and forgive anyone who offends me. I will remember that the Lord forgave me, so I must forgive others. Above all, I will clothe myself with love, which binds us all together in perfect harmony. And I will let the peace that comes from Christ rule in my heart. For as members of one body we are called to live in peace. And always be thankful.

Repeating verses like these while looking yourself in the eye will challenge you. But please do not think that you have set yourself up for failure by putting your sights on such a noble—and seemingly impossible—way to live. God never said you would have to do it all by yourself. In fact, by invoking the Word of God, you are calling on Jesus to live through you as you obey Him in baby steps. When you and I "put to death the sinful, earthly things lurking within us," we create space, making room for new things that God has for us. Dr. Henry Cloud says, "Faith requires stepping into a vacuum."[20] It isn't faith to stay surrounded by props that keep us safe.

Faith needs the space for a free fall.

Ask the Holy Spirit what you can surrender in your life. Let Him create space. But when your arms are finally open and free, be careful not to instinctively reach for what someone else has.

We tend to fill empty spaces. However, it is best to rid our arms of what we are carrying from the past—blame and regret—*as well as* what we are carrying in the present—jealousy and frustration— so that we can embrace our own divine calling. Paul says that the "secret" to embracing our divine calling is not willpower or a resolute mind. It is, very simply, that we "can do all things through Christ who strengthens [us]."[21] What you will find, as the Spirit lives in and through you more and more, is that you are finally free from the weight of the life that used to hinder you.

God called the space He created between the upper and lower waters *sky.*

He calls the space He creates between the soul and spirit *freedom.*

FOUR

Freedom

I FEEL THE INNER WAR every day. I desire to obey *and* I desire to live my own way. Most of the time, those are two different paths. The apostle Paul writes of the struggle here, and if we think of a human as having a distinctly separate soul and spirit, then these somewhat convoluted verses come into focus:

> I don't really understand myself, for I want to do what is right, but I don't do it. Instead, I do what I hate. But if I know that what I am doing is wrong, this shows that I agree that the law is good. So I am not the one doing wrong; it is sin living in me that does it.
>
> And I know that nothing good lives in me, that is, in my sinful nature. I want to do what is right, but I can't. I want to do what is good, but I don't. I don't want to do what is wrong, but I do it anyway. But if I do what I don't want to do, I am not really the one doing wrong; it is sin living in me that does it.[22]

Call it the *soul*, the *flesh*, the *sin nature*, whatever you want, but instinctively you can sense that there is a part of you wanting to stand up and take action in your world, and a part of you wanting to sit down and eat pizza on your couch. Part of you is ready to engage in the project that has been burning in your heart for years, and part of you gets caught up in another evening scrolling through social media. Part of you pulls toward something great, and part of you ignores that tug over and over again. These two sides of you are at war, and recognizing that there is, indeed, a conflict is the first step to conquering it. The people who do not admit this may have to take a longer route to victory in Jesus.

Let's aim to end the conflict quickly and avoid as many casualties as possible. One of the reasons that we may neglect to overcome some of the long-standing struggles in our lives is because we have been trying to motivate the wrong component of our beings: our soul.

But that didn't work for Paul. Whatever his concern, he was never able to conquer it from his soul. Even though he *wanted* to do what was right, he couldn't. This inability to make progress by way of the soul is what caused him to cry, "What a wretched man I am! Who will rescue me from this body that is subject to death?"[23]

But this is not to say that progress cannot be made. It just won't be made by reigning from the soul. Our only hope is that the transformation of the body is offered through the Spirit, and so "we do not lose courage. Though our outer self is heading for decay, our inner self is being renewed daily."[24]

Our soul is our humanity. Our soul is the flesh, and Jesus says, "Flesh gives birth to flesh."[25] Our hearts, minds, and wills cannot manufacture new life. We know that a human's reproductive system will always just produce another human, never a ferret. But why do we keep expecting our flesh to give birth to something other than more flesh?

It won't *ever* make a new and better you.

Yet, Jesus says, "the Spirit gives birth to spirit."[26] The Holy Spirit reproduces Himself. That is the very definition of new life. This is why we need the Word of God to divide between soul and spirit, so that we can focus on the life of the Spirit within us, nourishing and nurturing our spirit health with greater urgency than we nourish and nurture our mental or emotional health, which is only soul health. Soul health is important, even as body health is important, but ultimately, neither will lead to regeneration in us.

On the Second Day of Creation, when God divided water from water and created space, He was making room for the things He was about to bring into being. He was making the very area within which human, plant, and animal life would thrive. In the same way, when the Word of God divides soul from spirit in us, it creates space. God makes room for the things He is about to bring into being in our lives. The main thing He longs to bring to us is freedom itself.

Picture the other familiar time when God divided the waters and made space. In Exodus 14, God led His people out of bondage by splitting the Red Sea on their behalf. They traveled through the space He made for them on their way to even more freedom.

In this cluttered and overworked age, we long for freedom. Therefore, we must safeguard spiritual space. Safeguarding spiritual space is not about defending freedom for ourselves to enjoy. It is about defending freedom for God to move, to bring new things— to bring the *right* things—into our lives. We safeguard spiritual space through the spiritual disciplines, which are simple and time-proven practices that we can engage in regularly. Throughout this book, I will give you many examples of how I integrate the spiritual disciplines in my life.

For you, the idea of pursuing the spiritual disciplines may produce everything *but* freedom. It can feel mighty heavy to carry the burden of "something more to do." You may feel as if you hardly have time to read the Bible as it is, let alone take on additional avenues of spiritual transformation. But remember that God uses the Word as a sword that divides. Where He makes space, He creates room for things. He doesn't cram obligations into our lives the way we cram our dry cleaning into the closet. By His miraculous power, He will make space in your life you never thought you had. Embracing the spiritual disciplines will not burden your life, it will eliminate the unnecessary components in it.

Spiritual disciplines either add or subtract something from our lives in order to bless us. Some of the disciplines of addition are Bible reading/study, worship, prayer, soul friendship, reflection/journaling, celebration/feasting, and service. Some of the disciplines of subtraction are solitude, fasting, meditation, sacrifice/giving, rest, submission, and confession.

These practices do not require special aptitude; they are a means of grace, an access point to hear the heartbeat of heaven. The danger is that these disciplines can be a source of pride and become habitual. The blessing is that they give the Holy Spirit room to work. I am compelled to continue in these practices by something I heard flow out of my own mouth to children recently.

I kept hearing students in my class ask me two questions constantly, whether they were completing a drawing or writing a paragraph or preparing a poster or working math problems:

"Is this good?"

"Is this right?"

At first I was suckered into the trap. I wanted to assure their little hearts that they were on the right track. They wanted so badly to please me. But the more I answered their questions with, "Yes, that is good," and "Yes, you are doing it right," the more I realized I was weakening them, not strengthening them. I was creating dependents. They couldn't make a move without my approval.

You know that feeling when kids are pushing your buttons? We typically use that idiom to mean someone is doing something over and over again, and eventually they get an overreaction or an irritated response from us. It usually means something negative happens when a student says or does a certain thing.

I have tried to turn that idiom into something positive in my life. When I am becoming annoyed with a specific student behavior, I often ask God for a "push-button phrase" for me as a teacher. This is not a generic answer, such as "Because I said so." That kind of response just creates distrust between adults and children. Instead, I seek push-button phrases that will dispense life every time they are spoken. I prayed about the push-button answer for "Is this right?" and "Is this good?" and I came to: "It's not about right or wrong. It's not about good or bad. It's about practice." It took many times of responding to their requests for approval with this three-sentence answer, but eventually they stopped asking and felt secure.

This push-button phrase is *exactly* what we need to tell ourselves concerning the spiritual disciplines. Remember that the purpose of these practices is *practice*. Our focus is not to *do* more but to *be* more. The disciplines are a means of becoming like Christ. These are the things He did. As you incorporate His ways into your life in greater measure, hold on to the simple words of Philippians 4:9: "Keep *putting into practice* all you learned and received from me—everything you heard from me and saw me doing. Then the God of peace will be with you" (NLT, emphasis mine).

If you are reading this and shaking your head, thinking, *There is no way. Just no way. I do not have time anywhere in my schedule for this*, then another key problem in your life is revealing itself. In an earlier chapter, if you were not able to look yourself in the eye and read out loud what God says about you, it showed that your thoughts were not in agreement with His. In this chapter, if you are not able to shift your schedule in order to put God first, it shows that your time is not in alignment with His. So any amount of trying to fix a problem in your life has never worked because you have been trying fix the wrong problem. Misaligned thinking and mismanaged time are two giants that should be fought before any others.

Thinking as He thinks and doing as He does are two standards that must be established at once. Summarize your effort this way: put Him first.

Recently, one of the spiritual disciplines created a wide path of freedom in my life. Remember I said earlier that I have bitten my fingernails my entire life? My nail biting was constant. I thought it would be a shameful compulsion for the rest of my life. I never expected the problem would be instantly solved the way it was.

I was at a church service, and the teaching happened to focus on confession. The pastor explained confession in a clear way: Confession is agreement with God. It is looking at your life and agreeing with God about the things He wants to be removed or changed.

Sure, I always get around to obeying eventually. But sometimes I hesitate awhile, thinking it over first. I tell myself I'm just delaying, not disobeying. During that sermon, I thought of a specific area in which I had delayed and not obeyed.

But the Bible is clear: "Remember, it is sin to know what you ought to do and then not do it."[27]

The Bible is also clear that sin is not the final stop in the departure from God. Satan would never let us stop there.

God offers a command, any command, as a starting point for us. When a child of God veers from that, the book of James says he "is being tempted whenever he is being dragged off and enticed by the bait of his own desire. Then, having conceived, the desire gives birth to sin; and when sin is fully grown, it gives birth to death."[28] So the journey away from God does not lead to sin; it leads to *death*. That makes sense. God is Life, so to move away from Him is to move toward death. Death is the final stop. Sin is just a landmark along the way.

My delaying was disobeying, and my disobedience was sin. So I chose to confess.

Then I went home and did what God asked me to do. Immediately.

Weeks later, I looked at my hands and noticed that I had stopped biting my nails. Now I believe there is a connection to my confession.

Confession and agreement put us in position to receive God's best for our lives. How do I know? Read some more from James and see if you see what I see:

> Temptation comes from our own desires, which entice us and drag us away. These desires give birth to sinful actions. And when sin is allowed to grow, it gives birth to death.
>
> So don't be misled, my dear brothers and sisters. Whatever is good and perfect is a gift coming down to us from God our Father, who created all the lights in the heavens. He never changes or casts a shifting shadow. He

chose to give birth to us by giving us his true word. And we, out of all creation, became his prized possession.[29]

We were created to be His prized possession and to operate in agreement with our Creator, from whom every good gift comes. He hasn't changed since the day He gave us the gift of life. "I have come that they may have life, and have it to the full," Jesus assures us.[30] He is ever and always about *life*. When He speaks to us, He is giving "birth to us by giving us his true word." Whenever we hear His voice through His written Word or through His whispered word, then we must obey, knowing that He is speaking in order to birth something new, to bring regeneration to us. But we have to stay in agreement and in alignment with God to receive it. To confess is to calibrate our thoughts with His. "Whatever is good and perfect is a gift coming down to us" from above, right? Picture a waterfall over our heads. Well, the enemy wants to "entice us and drag us away" from that blessed downpour, causing us to step out from under the flow of life and goodness. To confess is to realign. It is to step back into the stream.

Deliverance from a nervous habit like nail biting was part of the goodness that God was willing to pour out on me through His Spirit. I had prayed about it many times over the years, but there were also many times over the years that I disobeyed His requests in various ways. If I refused to do what God asked me to do, how *could* He do what I was asking Him to do? I was not standing in a place where I could receive anything from Him.

This year confession took on yet *another* dimension for me. I had started experiencing negative effects in some relationships that were meaningful to me. I could find no real explanation for it, so I took the problem to Clint, one of my mentors, to see if he had any insight. He said it was easy to see the problem. I was reaping what I had sown. He suggested that I take a close look at what I had planted in those relationships in the last year.

When I truly became honest with myself, I saw that I had treated everyone involved as if they weren't important to me, when they actually were. I was afraid of looking too desperate to them and had pulled back again and again, behaving nonchalantly when my heart really wanted to be "all in."

"There you go. You found the seeds," he said. "So if you acted like those people didn't matter to you all year, no wonder *they* are acting like you don't matter to them now. That is the harvest you could have predicted."

I cried out, "Wow! I see that! But what do I do now?"

He smiled, putting his hand on my shoulder, and said, "You gotta harrow the fields."

Clint is an entrepreneur who has had many business endeavors, including farming. He explained to me that there were times when he and his business partners would plant fields and then see a less-than-desirable yield slowly start to come up out of the ground. The moment they realized it was going to be a bad crop, they knew time was of the essence. They had to replant while they still could. So they would attach a harrow to the tractor and harrow the fields. A harrow rips up the first few layers of soil, destroying anything that was planted previously. After the fields were harrowed, they could replant the ground with better seed.

As we ended our coffee shop mentoring session that day, he told me to search "harrowing" online and watch a few videos of fields being ripped up before we met again. "That's the kind of work you have to do, Nika. You have to undo what you did and then do something better. Don't blame everything on other people. Get to work planting better seed yourself."

Later, I watched a few videos and cried. I was truly sorrowful that I had planted bad seed in my relationships with my feigned indifference. This is how I harrowed the fields: I chose a different friend who was uninvolved in the situation, confessed how I had behaved, and committed to her that I would behave differently from then on. There are times when we should confess to a friend who is unrelated to the problem. The persons directly involved will still be the beneficiaries of our good confession, even if they do not hear it. I want to emphasize that this also can be used as a cop-out, so we must be careful. We should always ask God if we should confess directly to the party involved in our mistake. However, there are times when confessing to that person is unnecessary. An example would be when someone in my life came up to me once and said, "I have to apologize to you for ignoring you and being inconsiderate to you for the last twenty years. Something you did way back when we met made me angry, and I have been disliking you all this time. Please forgive me."

I was stunned.

He and I did not see one another often, so on the rare occasions when we had interacted, I had thought we were just fine. It kind of hurt my feelings to find out he had been harboring animosity toward me the whole time. So I was in shock on the day he confessed to me, then I hugged and forgave him, thinking, *Really, I could have gone the rest of my life without knowing that he has disliked me for twenty years.* I bet if he had asked God about whether to confess to me or to someone else, God might have told him to confess to someone else and then just start treating me right. (By the way, this never applies to marriage. You *must* confess to your spouse and not to someone else, because you are one flesh.)

Godly sorrow is one thing, but guilt is another. The difference is that one leads to life. We can be sure that "godly sorrow brings repentance that leads to salvation and leaves no regret, but worldly sorrow brings death."[31] Guilt produces death.

Let me take a moment here to address a common misconception. There is nothing, absolutely nothing, that removes sin and its effects except the application of Christ's blood. We apply His blood through agreement with Him by confession. Time and distance do not erase sin. Just because it has been many years since your sin, it does not mean that the sin is gone. It will continue to produce death until you harrow the fields.

A perfect example of this truth is in marriage. I am involved in a marriage support ministry where I pray for couples who are experiencing the beginnings of marriage failure. They want to repair and restore their marriage but don't know how. Over time I have seen a pattern in praying with them. Ninety-nine percent of the couples I meet who are in marriage distress lived with one another or had sex with one another before they were in the covenant of marriage. God is clear that this is sin. The couple knew this. And so they got married, which they think remedied the problem of their sin. They think that they set themselves right in God's eyes by entering a covenant and approaching physical intimacy His way.

Listen to me, and please hear me saying this with an outpouring of love for you: your sin has not been rectified by getting married, because marriage does not rectify sin. That is a lie that you may have believed. And it doesn't matter how long ago you got married either; the seeds you planted years ago are still there. They are still producing a bad crop. It is only a matter of time until you see it. As we have learned from the progression of sin, that bad crop will get worse and worse until it produces death, perhaps the death of your marriage. I am not writing this so that you will feel guilt. Guilt leads to death faster than anything else. I am writing this so that you will experience godly sorrow, which leads to repentance and leaves no regret. I want you to move forward in peace and joy and life with no regret.

You may be reading this and saying, "We slept together before we got married, but we don't have any problems in our marriage."

All I can say is that this is a dangerous response.

The appropriate action, if you have old sin in your marriage (or in your business dealings, or in any area of your life), is to harrow the fields. Examine the seeds you have planted in the past, and ask God to help you rip them out of the fertile ground of your heart. Then agree with Him through confession. Choose a soul friend (regarding sex outside of marriage, that person will be your spouse) and confess that you agree with God that what He says is sin is, indeed, sin. Only the application of Christ's blood through agreeing with Him rectifies sin, not time, distance, money, marriage, or anything else.

Here is the good news: in the cases of the people I have prayed for in the last few years, all of these couples reaped an incredible harvest in their marriage after they harrowed the lies and sowed truth. They didn't even know how good the crop could be when the bad seeds were finally gone from it.

Practices like confession acknowledge something mysterious: we are people living new lives in the Spirit, and "since we live by the Spirit, let us keep in step with the Spirit."[32] The cascade of good and perfect gifts never stops, but we must stay under the flow. Our fleshly ideas of how to fix things will never work.

I understand my habits in a new way now. I do not seek to solve them myself but look to the Spirit in me to author new life when I am headed in the opposite direction. The other day I noticed a strong urge to bite my nails again. Instead of condemning myself or fighting the impulse with my heart, mind, and will, I took a break, became silent for ten minutes, and then prayed. Both silence and prayer are spiritual disciplines that help us align with the Source of Life. During those moments, He doesn't always say what we expect Him to say. I went to Him for encouragement to resist temptation. In an answer to my request, He did not say, *You can do it, Nika!*

Instead, He answered quickly, *Do you trust Me?*

I knew what He meant. I was approaching the deadline for a book and had fallen behind. I felt my nervous habits creeping back because I had put the responsibility and pressure for the completed project on myself instead of giving my "burdens to the LORD." He promises that if I do, "He will not permit the godly to slip and fall."[33]

Looking to myself for answers keeps my eyes on the flesh, and—I'll say it again—flesh only gives birth to flesh. New life is found in the Spirit alone, and spiritual disciplines are the way we stay aligned with Him.

When we see symptoms of anxiety and unrest in our lives, we should ask the Lord if they are symptoms of disobedience. We can't blame God when our own choices pulled us out of the flow of blessings.

Confession puts us back in position.

Space and freedom in our lives *can* still be accomplished with just a word. When we agree with *the* Word, then it does what God sent it to do—divides soul and spirit.

Freedom creates room for things. And when there is room for things, blessings finally have a place to land.

The Third Day, Morning

Then God said, "Let the waters beneath the sky flow
together into one place, so dry ground may appear."
And that is what happened. God called the dry ground "land"
and the waters "seas." And God saw that it was good.

—

GENESIS 1:9–10 NLT

Like an artist with an array of oil paints, the Creator sweeps a palette knife across the blank canvas of the world. With the edge of the knife, He scrapes the sea to the side, and the violet pile of water deepens, darkens, with every inch He pushes it back. Now an ocean stands on one side of the blade.

The oceans have their purpose.

On the other side of the knife, dry ground, the face of the canvas, appears for the first time. God is not finished. His wrist turns, and suddenly rivers run— a vivid azure—cutting through the virgin terrain.

The rivers have their purpose.

Then the Artist blends a murky blue-green and drops it into a valley.

A lake.

A few miles away, He does it again, but smaller this time.

A pond.

The lakes have their purpose. And so do the ponds.

"Let the waters beneath the sky flow into place," He says.

On Day Three, God orders the waters to make room for land.

FIVE

Let There Be Order

GOD POSITIONED THE WATERS so that they could fulfill their purpose. He planned to fill the waters with hidden gifts. These hidden gifts were for His children to find. He planned gifts for our sense of taste, like sea salt, and lobster, and catfish. He planned gifts for our sense of touch, like coral, and conch shells, and an orca's skin. He planned gifts for our sense of sight, like the metallic back of a swordfish, and the neon shine of a jellyfish, and the lunar glow of pearls. He planned gifts for our sense of hearing, like the snicker of a dolphin, and the moan of a whale, and the whisper of the surf. He planned gifts for our sense of smell, like brine, and musk, and the tang of seaweed.

It is so obvious. The gifts God gave the waters were not for the sake of the waters, so the waters do not keep them. The gifts He gave the waters were for *us*.

Stop and think about how this could translate from nature to humanity.

The LORD directs the steps of the godly.
    He delights in every detail of their lives.[1]

If God is going to direct our steps, then we must take a step in the first place. Too many of us feel the pull of purpose within us but never move into it. We think there will be a miraculous opening of the way before us, like the Red Sea before Moses, revealing dry ground. Sometimes that happens. But more often, the way opens before us like the Jordan River before Joshua. God directed Joshua and his men to move into the waters while the river raged at flood stage. The dry ground appeared only after they put their feet into the flood. As soon as they took action, God pushed back the waters.

Their miracle required a step.[2]

God orders our lives—positioning us as we take steps—so that we can fulfill our purpose.

How do we know our purpose? Well, knowing our purpose is the easy part. If we have completely surrendered our lives to Christ, then we have been crucified, and we no longer live, but Christ lives in us.[3] He lives in us and now He lives out His purpose through us. That is why we can cling to the truth of Romans 8:28: "And we know that all things work together for good to those who love God, to those who are the called according to His purpose" (NKJV).

Knowing our purpose is not even about our purpose, really.

It's about *His* purpose: "I have come so that they may have life, life in its fullest measure."[4]

Jesus's purpose is to sustain life, the same as the oceans, rivers, lakes, and ponds are purposed to sustain life. It makes perfect sense. He is the Living Water. Look for a moment at the way He introduces Himself in a conversation.

He stops to rest at a well, and a woman who has had several sour relationships comes to draw water. Jesus does the unspeakable. He kindly asks her for a drink, which surprises her, because she expects Jesus to be like every other man she has known. By now she assumes she will be treated like trash.

He asks her for the drink, yes, but then tells her the tables should be turned. (Jesus likes to turn over tables wherever He goes.) "*If you only knew the gift God has for you* and who you are speaking to," He says to her, "you would ask me, and I would give you living water."[5]

The woman wants it, just like we do, and asks where to get it. Jesus is quick to divide soul and spirit, lest she think what's in her bucket would do the trick.

Anyone who drinks this water will soon become thirsty again. [See the way He refers to the soul, or human effort?] But those who drink the water I give will never be thirsty again. [There it is, the Spirit.] It becomes a fresh, bubbling spring within them, giving them eternal life.[6]

Well, it seems clear as a woodland stream, but just to make sure we understand what He means, let's double-check His definition of Living Water.

Anyone who is thirsty may come to me! Anyone who believes in me may come and drink! For the Scriptures declare, "Rivers of living water will flow from his heart." (When he said "living water," he was speaking of the Spirit, who would be given to everyone believing in him.)[7]

Our purpose is to sustain life (ahem . . . and not just our *own*). Now, how does He order our lives so that we can fulfill our purpose? He places us in different locations and gives us different opportunities and experiences, all so that we can offer the gifts that He has hidden within us.

Are you with me? When Jesus said to the woman, "If only you knew the gift God has for you," He was referring to the Spirit, and to the gifts of the Spirit, which bring abundant life.

The spiritual gifts God gave us are not only for the sake of ourselves, so we do not keep them hidden. The gifts He gave us are for *others*.

Now, an exploration of the spiritual gifts is a little bit like diving into the Atlantic. We could find ourselves in deep water pretty quickly. Clarifying the difference between disciplines and gifts will help. Whereas spiritual *disciplines* are the ways Christ works with the Spirit to transform us, spiritual *gifts* are the ways Christ works through us to transform the world.

There is no better way to explain this than by introducing you to my friend Ann. If you asked *her*, Ann would say she is a pond. She would tell you she exercises her gifts in very small and meaningful ways. But if you asked *me*, I would tell you that she is more like an ocean, because the small things she does have the impact of a tidal wave.

Let's meet her right in the middle of her typical day.

As she wipes the glass cleaner from the mirror, Ann smiles. She loves her job of keeping the church building clean on Sundays. Praise songs echo from the auditorium, and in another half hour, happy children will be running through the halls, eager to show off their crafts from Bible class. Sundays are always a pleasant day to work.

Then the door behind her bursts open, and she looks up to see a woman run into the bathroom with her head down. Even without the mirror's reflection, Ann can tell the woman is crying. The woman rushes into a stall, sits down, and sobs.

"It was Mother's Day," Ann tells me, tears filling her own eyes. "Mother's Day can be hard sometimes. Whether she had lost her mother, or lost her child, or wanted a child, I never knew. I didn't want to bother her and I didn't want to leave her there all by herself, so I just stayed and prayed while I cleaned the rest of the bathroom. For thirty minutes, she cried without stopping. It broke my heart. We may not know another person's story, but God does. Prayer is always something we can do to help."

When the woman finally comes out of the stall, Ann is waiting. She asks the woman if she needs anything, any kind of assistance. Crying anew, the woman says nothing, but she accepts Ann's embrace before drying her eyes and returning to the church service.

Heart care may not be part of the job description for most persons in custodial services, but it is for Ann. Especially now that she works on a college campus.

"It was on that Mother's Day years ago that I decided to pray over bathroom stalls, because people go into them for all different reasons we will never know," she says. "Now I pray as I clean. By doing that, I can positively influence every single person on this campus, every single day, because a bathroom is the one place that everybody will be at one time or another."

Hear the sermon from a cleaning cart: it is not the work you do that matters, but the *purpose* you see in the work you do.

Ann admits that there have been a few humorous interactions since the students found out she was praying for them in the bathroom every day.

"It made me laugh when one girl came up to me and said, 'Hey, Ann! I have a big final exam in a few minutes. Do you think you can pray over the stall I am about to use? I need all the help I can get!'" Ann says she took the hand of the sophomore, quietly praying right there by the sink.

When I ask her if janitorial work ever drags on or becomes difficult, she quickly brushes the thought aside. Her workday goes quickly and is almost always fun because, to her, working is more than just work. It is her way of showing that she cares. "I am not just cleaning. I am keeping a clean environment so that people can learn and grow. If I stopped doing what I do, they would notice. I know my work is important, and so do they. The students show me they love me and are thankful for me. I get hugs from them all day long."

Ann leans forward and grins as she throws in one last bit of wisdom. "Work isn't hard when you know you are loved."

My dear friend Ann's spiritual gift is service, and through it, she reminds us that any work can be our greatest mission if we decide it will be. She is the embodiment of one of my favorite lines from the classic movie *Chariots of Fire*: "You can praise God by peeling a spud, if you peel it to perfection."[8]

More of us should view our work as worship. Perhaps we don't because somewhere in the backs of our minds, we feel alone when we work. And because we feel alone, we have our own scales by which we evaluate whether the work we are doing is having a significant impact in the world.

There are several problems with this viewpoint. First, we are not alone. When God gives us a task, He doesn't expect us to do it by ourselves. In Haggai 2:4, we read this exhortation: "'And now get to work, for I am with you,' says the LORD of the Heaven's Armies" (NLT). When God sends us to work, He doesn't send us alone; He goes with us. And He might even bring His army with Him.

The second problem with our general view of personal purpose is that we think we should choose work based upon our interests and values. This is where the days of Creation become paramount in our search for meaningful influence. If we believe that God created us, then we must believe He created us for *His* purpose. Do we have any doubt about this after reading these verses?

> For we are God's handiwork, created in Christ Jesus to do good works, which God prepared in advance for us to do.[9]

> God, who began the good work within you, will continue his work until it is finally finished on the day when Christ Jesus returns.[10]

> And whatever you do or say, do it as a representative of the Lord Jesus, giving thanks through him to God the Father.[11]

> Work willingly at whatever you do, as though you were working for the Lord rather than for people.[12]

> But who are you, a human being, to talk back to God? "Shall what is formed say to the one who formed it, 'Why did you make me like this?'"[13]

God made us, so He knows how and why He made us. He filled us with hidden gifts. In the same way that He set the borders of the waters and made all bodies of water necessary to sustain life, He ordered you and me, and made all of us necessary in the Kingdom.

What we do matters. The place doesn't. We can worship in the sanctuary, in the mountains, or in the workplace. Purpose is connected to praise. We see that in Ann's life as she cleans to the glory of God. More importantly, we hear Jesus teaching this to the woman at the well. She wants to know where to worship, in Jerusalem or on a mountain. Jesus tells her,

> A time is coming and has now come when the true worshipers will worship the Father in the Spirit and in truth, for they are the kind of worshipers the Father seeks. God is spirit, and his worshipers must worship in the Spirit and in truth.[14]

What does it mean to worship in the Spirit? It means to recognize that He is within us at all times, calling us to reflect Him, as if we were a still pool of water with hidden gifts underneath.

The verses that you can write down and read out loud as you look yourself in the eye will bless you as you uncover those hidden gifts.

Let There Be Purpose
(from 1 Corinthians 12:4–11 NLT)

I, _____, know that there are different kinds of spiritual gifts, but the same Spirit is the source of them all. There are different kinds of service, but we serve the same Lord. God works in different ways, but it is the same God who does the work in all of us.

A spiritual gift is given to each of us, including me, so we can help each other. To one person the Spirit gives the ability to give wise advice; to another the same Spirit gives a message of special knowledge. The same Spirit gives great faith to another, and to someone else the one Spirit gives the gift of healing. He gives one person the power to perform miracles, and another the ability to prophesy. He gives someone else the ability to discern whether a message is from the Spirit of God or from another spirit. Still another person is given the ability to speak in unknown languages, while another is given the ability to interpret what is being said. It is the one and only Spirit who distributes all these gifts. He alone decides which gift each person should have.

We worship everywhere in everything when we bring forth the spiritual gifts that are within us.

And if you have not yet discovered your hidden gift, then picture Jesus looking into your eyes right now the same way He looked at the woman at the well. He winks as He whispers, *If only you knew the gift God has for you.*

For some of us, the first step in discovering our gifts is believing that God has given them to us in the first place.

SIX

Purpose

IT IS POSSIBLE for us to move in a thousand different directions when we are not convinced of our purpose. Our lives seem scattered. Maybe you feel this way. You have a sense that God has placed you here on Earth to do something, but you don't know what it is. You hear people talking about their passion and you aren't sure you have one. You consider dozens of possibilities that could work, and all of them are appealing. But you can't do them all. And if you can't do them all, then how do you go about choosing just one? You know that God has an important task for you, but you don't even have a long-distance lens to begin to spot that task on the horizon of your future.

Allow me to escort you toward discovery. Perhaps your *motivational* spiritual gift can serve as the lens you have been longing for. Knowing your go-to gifts can bring your purpose into focus.

Here is what I mean by a go-to gift. My mother has a go-to wedding shower gift. It is a sturdy iron skillet. Everybody needs an iron skillet, but few people register for one, she says. While she claims that there is no wedding gift more practical for a cook than an iron skillet, I surmise that the practicality falls a little more on her side of the gift wrap. She knows where the iron skillets are in the store, and she can get one in a hurry without having to make a decision about it.

But please do not think that just because she has identified her go-to gift, and because it is easy for her to give, it is less of a gift to others. I think an iron skillet is an excellent gift. Nothing puts a crispy edge on biscuits like baking them in an iron skillet instead of on a cookie sheet. It brings out vibrant flavor in sautéed vegetables too.

There is an important lesson we can learn from my mother's skillet: knowing your go-to gift makes giving it easier.

And knowing your purpose makes living it easier.

Recently, I was reading through several studies about spiritual gifts and realized that I had been putting all the spiritual gifts together into one amorphous lump for most of my life. The information I learned through the Institute in Basic Life Principles completely changed my understanding. Discovering that there could be three categories of spiritual gifts reduced the confusion for me.

- *Motivational* gifts refer to the way God works in believers' thoughts to help them see the world.
- *Ministry* gifts refer to the way God works with believers' actions to help them serve the world.
- *Manifestation* gifts refer to the way God works through believers' thoughts and actions to supernaturally touch the world with Himself.

All three types of gifts are given to us to build up the church and to reach others who need Christ.[15]

Let's consider motivational gifts. It is important that you recognize the motivational gift the Spirit has hidden in you, because it offers an overarching perspective that affects how you see the world and how you see yourself. Your motivational gift shapes your vision. You may have gone many years without identifying this gift in yourself, but the enemy hasn't gone one day without recognizing it. He can tell through your words and actions that a certain gift is motivating you, and he plans to exploit what God has given you. He wants to use it to harm instead of to bless. The Lord uses this motivational gift to direct you in positive ways, but the enemy uses the very same gift to direct you in negative ways. Therefore, knowing your motivation not only gives you an awareness of your go-to gift to give others, it also gives you an awareness of the primary strategies that the enemy will employ against you. On top of this, knowing not only *your* motivational gift but the motivational gifts of your loved ones will enrich and protect your relationships.

Get ready to love this.

But you must believe something as we start: God has given *everyone* a motivational gift. Everyone. He has not left you out. It may help you to take a quick survey of the motivational gifts in order to discern yours. Before you begin, pray and ask the Holy Spirit to instruct you. As you seek to know the truth about how you were made, the Holy Spirit will lead you into that truth.[16] Guiding people into truth is what He does.

Next, read through the seven descriptions and choose one that resonates with you. You might have several characteristics from each description, but select one of the seven descriptions that *best* describes you. I have labeled the gifts with letters to keep them disguised until later.

GIFT A:

1. You are committed to facilitating justice for others.
2. You sometimes feel you are convicted by God to take bold or confrontational action.
3. You are willing to speak up, especially about right and wrong.
4. You are bothered if you see wrongdoing and then say nothing about it.
5. You can evaluate people and situations quickly.
6. You have a "feeling" about whether someone or something is trustworthy.
7. You value truth.
8. You have a strong reaction when you sense dishonesty.
9. You deeply desire that people and situations come to justice.
10. You are transparent about your own personal flaws in the name of total honesty.
11. You are sold out once you have committed to a person or situation.
12. You are fiercely loyal, so you have only a small number of relationships you consider to be close.
13. You put truth first, even if you have to put truth before people.
14. You are articulate and eager to help people understand what is true and right.
15. You enjoy seeing a relationship between two people or a relationship between a person and God be restored.
16. You do not compromise or take shortcuts when it comes to the Bible or human laws.
17. You are not easily swayed by emotions.
18. You stand up for what is right, even when it hurts.

19. You are troubled by relativity; you easily accept that there are absolutes.
20. Your highest joy is helping people operate with integrity.

GIFT B:

1. You are committed to using your hands to bless others.
2. You sometimes feel useless if you are not busy doing or helping.
3. You are willing to work harder than anyone else if it benefits your family or group.
4. You are bothered when your work is not acknowledged. You like knowing if your work mattered.
5. You can see what needs to be done immediately.
6. You have a "feeling" about what would make someone's day.
7. You value a good work ethic.
8. You have a strong reaction when you see people not doing all that they can.
9. You feel great joy in taking care of the needs of others so that they can be successful.
10. You keep working to finish a task you have begun, even when you are exhausted.
11. You are good at many things.
12. You find it hard to say no when people ask for your help.
13. You love adding that "special touch."
14. You show you care by remembering birthdays and anniversaries, favorite colors and foods, or special preferences of those you love.
15. You like helping in immediate ways or with short-range projects; you feel frustrated by long and ongoing plans.
16. You feel better when things are in order.

17. You like to do more than is expected, and you pay attention to details.
18. You don't like to delegate.
19. You like to meet needs efficiently so you often just go ahead and use your personal funds rather than wait on a committee's decision about resources.
20. Your highest joy is helping people by serving them in special ways.

GIFT C:

1. You are committed to validating information for others.
2. You are careful about those you listen to. You like to know a speaker's background and credentials. You think it is important for others to know your background and credentials when you speak or offer advice.
3. You turn to reliable resources to validate information you read or hear.
4. You like to present information in an orderly sequence. You like an argument to be laid out logically.
5. You enjoy research and fact-finding. You enjoy gathering and analyzing information.
6. You like to provide details that others often miss. You feel secure when you have all the details about a situation.
7. You value facts above opinions or experiences. You prefer to deal in objective rather than subjective details.
8. You remain loyal to certain instructors, churches, or schools that have your respect.
9. You want to clarify misunderstandings, and if you find out you were mistaken, you retrace your steps to find out where you went wrong. You want to help others do the same.

10. You are willing to read diligently to discover truth.

11. You are passionate about correcting error.

12. You faithfully study the Word of God.

13. You have excellent study habits.

14. You value knowledge.

15. You are analytical.

16. You make presentations in a systematic way.

17. You feel you must be thorough in giving the background information behind an action.

18. You are dependable.

19. You would rather not make a decision than make one without all of the details.

20. Your highest joy is helping people make a sound decision.

GIFT D:

1. You are committed to encouraging spiritual growth in others.

2. You can often discern the stumbling blocks to spiritual growth in others and desire to help them remove obstacles in order to experience freedom.

3. You point people to hope, telling testimonies from your life and from the lives of others.

4. You believe God works for our good, even through sorrow and suffering, and you eagerly direct others to faith and trust when they are hurting.

5. You desire transparency in the name of spiritual growth. You are vulnerable with others because you want to bring darkness into the light.

6. You have deep insights to share, as you have turned to Scripture during troublesome times in your life.

7. You see improvement and growth in clear logical steps, and when you explain them to others, you expect them to act quickly and begin.

8. You value face-to-face communication more than any other kind. You want to make eye contact and see the facial expressions of others as you communicate.

9. You encourage maturity in others.

10. You view trials as opportunities for growth.

11. You prefer to help someone spiritually rather than help them with a physical need.

12. You provide people with a biblical perspective of life.

13. You like coaching people.

14. You are willing and eager to come alongside and walk with someone who is hurting.

15. You value time spent meditating on or memorizing Scripture.

16. You want to invest in your own well of spiritual resources so that you will have it when you need it.

17. You see all things as a part of God's sovereign and loving plan.

18. You give thanks in all seasons and circumstances.

19. You often write or speak to inspire and encourage others.

20. Your highest joy is helping people experience victory.

GIFT E:

1. You are committed to giving financial resources to others.

2. You tend to make wise investments.

3. You are eager to share what you have, whether you have a little or a lot, but you want to be sure God is directing you to offer your resources in that area.

4. You like to save money.

5. You provide high-quality gifts. You want your gifts to have a lasting impact in someone's life.

6. You are bothered when a need is unmet.

7. You look to the Lord's guidance when you give, and you enjoy giving secretly.

8. You enjoy giving, but you are aware that sometimes gifts bring dependency in immature believers. You desire that your financial gifts be handled in such a way that does not bring corruption.

9. You are frugal and thrifty, knowing how to get the best buy.

10. You are sometimes considered "stingy" by your family because they see you delaying gratification in order to be generous later.

11. You want others to experience the joy of giving, and you encourage them to give.

12. You do not like to feel pressured into giving; you prefer to identify needs yourself.

13. You have an uncanny ability to accumulate resources.

14. You are a hard worker with conservative values in most respects.

15. You like to become personally involved in the lives of the people you support.

16. You dislike the idea of debt.

17. You find pleasure in choosing less costly ways of doing things.

18. You avoid waste by being careful with resources.

19. You like to confirm the amount you will give or the opportunity to give with another person.

20. Your highest joy is helping people by meeting a financial need.

GIFT F:

1. You are committed to the final outcome and to envisioning it for others.
2. You desire for those working with you to be dependable and devoted.
3. You would rather have a small team of trustworthy associates than a large team of people you are not completely sure of.
4. You share tasks well, knowing which tasks you must complete yourself.
5. You love seeing people grow in their work, as you delegate more complex assignments.
6. You are willing to endure pressure and some resistance from your team because you know the end result will be worth the effort.
7. You break down large goals into small, achievable steps.
8. You make difficult tasks look easy. You have been told that you can do impossible things.
9. You spot the vital components to completing a task.
10. You remove distractions and focus on what is essential to the ultimate goal.
11. You are efficient, using people and resources in the best possible ways.
12. You love placing people according to their strengths and weaknesses so that everyone can be successful.
13. You are decisive.
14. You evaluate an organization quickly and can see areas for improvement.
15. You are not satisfied if you are not working on a project.

16. You enjoy working with a strong team. You reward your team.
17. You use time wisely.
18. You take time away to make new goals and review your progress on previous ones.
19. You are thorough and see things through to the end.
20. Your highest joy is helping people complete a big job beautifully.

GIFT G:

1. You are committed to being empathetic toward others.
2. You need intimate, emotional relationships.
3. You are seen as being kind and gentle.
4. You can sense when others are hurting, and you feel their pain.
5. You find it difficult to be firm sometimes.
6. You do not want to offend or hurt anyone.
7. You value genuine love.
8. You are willing to be vulnerable, therefore sometimes you get hurt easily.
9. You are caring and compassionate, so people in need are drawn to you.
10. You value physical closeness.
11. You enjoy times of meaningful fellowship.
12. You love to pray and feel you *must* pray.
13. You want to be needed.
14. You tend to embrace humility.
15. You can sense the emotional atmosphere in a room.
16. You tend to reach out and get involved to offer support when someone is in need.

17. You can look past the outside and see the heart.
18. You are drawn to other sensitive people.
19. You often take up others' offenses.
20. Your highest joy is helping to comfort people in distress.

Hopefully one of these descriptions stood out to you. Continue praying for clarity if several seemed to fit. Although you may have several ministry gifts, more than likely the Lord will be shaping your vision of life and the world through *one* motivational gift. The more you can sense your go-to gift, the more you can see the ways God brings the scattered pieces in your experience into a unified purpose. He tends to draw you to Him and to the world through your motivational gift. Your motivational gift becomes a magnet.

If you identified with Gift A, then you may have the motivational gift of prophecy. Prophets are aware of untruth, and God blesses the church through you by exposing sin and spiritual compromise via your steadfast adherence to God's Word. Through you, He brings His justice to the world.

If you identified with Gift B, then you may have the motivational gift of service. Servers are aware of needs, and God blesses the church through you by meeting those needs via your tireless desire to be the hands and feet of Jesus. Through you, He brings His care to the world.

If you identified with Gift C, then you may have the motivational gift of teaching. Teachers are aware of inaccuracy, and God blesses the church through you by keeping details, doctrine, and principles aligned via your passion to have the mind of Christ. Through you, He brings His wisdom to the world.

If you identified with Gift D, then you may have the motivational gift of exhortation. Exhorters are aware of despair, and God blesses the church through you by encouraging believers to persevere and keep going via your faith in God's loving plan. Through you, He brings His hope to the world.

If you identified with Gift E, then you may have the motivational gift of giving. Givers are aware of deficit, and God blesses the church through you by using your resources via your desire to share God's abundance. Through you, He brings His provision to the world.

If you identified with Gift F, then you may have the motivational gift of leadership, which I like to refer to as the gift of organization. Organizers are aware of aimlessness, and God blesses the church through you by casting vision via your ability to see people and processes through God's eyes. Through you, He brings His direction to the world.

If you identified with Gift G, then you may have the motivational gift of mercy. Mercy givers are aware of pain, and God blesses the church through you by touching hurting people via your sensitivity to love with God's heart. Through you, He brings His comfort to the world.

We know that God has given us spiritual gifts to accomplish His purpose. For some believers, it is a stretch to consider what it means to give their spiritual gifts. The whole idea is intimidating, and they want to know what a go-to gift looks like in practical action. In order to know the result of the Spirit's gifts, we have to return to the description of the Spirit. He is Living Water. In the natural realm, water poured upon growing trees produces fruit. In the supernatural realm, Living Water poured upon growing hearts produces the fruit of the Spirit.

The beautiful thing about fruit is that it is filled with seeds. So what is produced will be reproduced. Your purpose won't stop with you.

The Third Day, Afternoon

Then God said, "Let the land produce vegetation:
seed-bearing plants and trees on the land that bear fruit
with seed in it, according to their various kinds."
And it was so. The land produced vegetation:
plants bearing seed according to their kinds and trees
bearing fruit with seed in it according to their kinds.
And God saw that it was good. And there was evening,
and there was morning—the third day.

—

GENESIS 1:11–13

The earth blossoms for the first time. It is a kaleidoscope of color. God shows His tenderness in the buttery petals of peonies, His vibrancy in the scarlet shock of poppies, and His perfection in the petite bells of lilies of the valley.

He spins zinnias. Ignites azaleas. Breathes Queen Anne's lace. Folds a bird-of-paradise plant like origami.

Next, He fashions fruit with great delight, hanging bananas high and twisting grapevine tendrils low. He buzzes the fuzz of a kiwi. Slices a pineapple's ponytail. He laughs and scatters berries.

He fills an orange. Wraps an apple in skin. Kisses the blushing cheek of a peach.

This is His Garden. The majesty of His mind manifested for all to see. His thoughts take on shape. He loves preparing Eden.

He will not stop until her beauty is a feast for the human soul. This is where He will walk with us.

He will not stop until her bounty is a feast for the human body. This is where He will dine with us.

"Let the land produce," He says.

On Day Three, God covers the land with seed-bearing plants and trees.

SEVEN

Let There Be Fruitfulness

IN FRUIT TREES, we see the pattern for His magnificent plan for people. He wants us to be so healthy in our communion with Him that we provide beauty to the world and nourishment for the Body, which is the church. The key to this ongoing, fruit-bearing health is trust.

> But blessed is the one who trusts in the LORD,
> whose confidence is in him.
> They will be like a tree planted by the water
> that sends out its roots by the stream.
> It does not fear when heat comes;
> its leaves are always green.
> It has no worries in a year of drought
> and never fails to bear fruit.[1]

We can see how important fruitfulness is to Jesus. Walking with His disciples one day, He hungrily reaches into the branches of a nearby fig tree, only to find there are no figs among the leaves.

He curses the tree, saying, "'May no one ever eat your fruit again!' And the disciples heard him say it."[2]

No word of the Bible is wasted. If this passage deliberately points out that *the disciples heard* how Jesus felt about fruitlessness, then it is significant. The curse was for the disciples to hear. The Master was conveying purpose: "I did not create trees to just sit around being trees. I made them to produce. So it is with *you*." We are designed to produce fruit. A lot of it. The divine sequence of re-creation has brought us from revelation, to freedom, to purpose, and now we have finally come to the phase we have been craving from the beginning: productivity. The kind of productivity that God values is fruit bearing. By fruit, He means the fruit of the Spirit.

So that we do not confuse similar terms, let's clarify one more time. Spiritual disciplines are the ways Christ works with the Spirit to transform us. Spiritual gifts are the ways Christ works through us to transform the world, including the church. Now we will look at the fruit of the Spirit, which are the godly character traits that the Holy Spirit produces in us when we practice spiritual disciplines and operate in spiritual gifts.

You will recognize the Spirit's fruit as love, joy, peace, patience, kindness, goodness, faithfulness, gentleness, and self-control.[3] Yet I would not want you to miss the delight of reading this lovely list as it is paraphrased in *The Message*. The Holy Spirit enables us to display the impossible:

> . . . things like affection for others, exuberance about life, serenity. We develop a willingness to stick with things, a sense of compassion in the heart, and a conviction that a basic holiness permeates things and people. We find ourselves involved in loyal commitments, not needing to

force our way in life, able to marshal and direct our energies wisely.

Abiding in Christ produces the fruit of the Spirit, which feeds *us* as well as those around us. Being well nourished means we will grow and perform at a high capacity, using our gifts in their strength instead of their weakness. Yet it is important to consider how the gifts God has given us can be used in their weakness because we will more easily spot the strategy of the enemy in our lives. What God intends for us to use, the enemy desires for us to misuse.

God wants our gifts to make us think more *like* the Savior. The enemy wants our gifts to make us think we *are* the savior. Let's look at some of the ways the enemy uses our gifts in their weak form.

If you are a *prophet* operating from weakness, you may:
- Expose someone without restoring them.
- Jump to conclusions.
- React harshly to people who compromise.
- Be unforgiving and end relationships with those who fail.
- Condemn yourself when you fail.
- Be prideful when you are right.
- Not be judicious about the best time and place to speak out.
- Make rash decisions.
- Have extreme opinions.
- Be intolerant.
- Rebuke without tact.
- Speak the truth without love.
- Dwell on the negative.
- Keep people dependent on your evaluation.

The Lord will use your gift of prophecy to restore people. The enemy will misuse your gift of prophecy to alienate people. In the enemy's hands, you will desire to be the one who always has the last word. Taken to extremes, prophets will alienate people until others look to you as the ultimate judge.

But the Judge is God, and He is the One who has the last word.

If you are a *server* operating from weakness, you may:

- Give unrequested help.
- Fulfill other peoples' needs while leaving your family's needs unmet.
- Put too much focus on details and being perfectionistic.
- Do things quickly yourself without waiting for input from others.
- Work beyond reasonable physical limits.
- Handle tasks that the Lord meant for others.
- Overreact to overlooked needs.
- Resent lack of appreciation from the recipients of your help.
- Prevent others from serving alongside you if they don't do things as well as you do and instead insist on doing it all yourself.
- Value the final product more than the fellowship and cooperation that could have gone into it.
- Become frustrated with time limits.
- Be demanding of others who are not working as you expect.
- Become irritated when people want to be involved with what you are doing for them, such as when they want to

know when things will be finished or ask to have a look too soon.
- Keep people dependent on your assistance.

The Lord will use your gift of serving to make people feel welcome. The enemy will misuse your gift of serving to make people feel dismissed. In the enemy's hands, you will desire to be the one who always saves the day. Taken to extremes, servers will dismiss people's help until others look to you as the ultimate helper.

But the Helper is God, and He is the One who saves the day.

If you are a *teacher* operating from weakness, you may:
- Become proud of knowledge.
- Despise lack of credentials.
- Depend on human reasoning.
- Show off research skills.
- Reject the idea that some things are understood by faith alone.
- Exalt reason above the Holy Spirit's leading.
- Take doctrine to the extreme.
- Argue over minor points.
- Disdain teachers who use illustrations instead of focusing on facts.
- Give more information than was asked for or needed.
- Question a person's presentation until they feel belittled.
- Dismiss a person's or group's feelings about something in favor of the facts about it.
- Obsessively search for information in order to make a decision, and postpone taking action until it is too late.
- Keep people dependent on your knowledge.

The Lord will use your gift of teaching to educate people. The enemy will misuse your gift of teaching to show people they are ignorant. In the enemy's hands, you will desire to be the one who always has all the answers. Taken to extremes, teachers will show people their ignorance until others look to you as the ultimate source of wisdom.

But the Source of wisdom is God, and He is the One with all the answers.

If you are an *exhorter* operating from weakness, you may:

- Keep family and friends waiting on you while you minister to others.
- Look to yourself for solutions and answers instead of to God.
- Take personal credit for results in the life of someone you are walking alongside.
- Jump headfirst into a new endeavor without thinking through the cost and without finishing the previous task.
- Treat people like spiritual-growth projects.
- Use illustrations from the lives of others and share stories they may have told you in confidence.
- Avoid doctrine that does not have immediate practical application.
- Oversimplify solutions.
- Set unrealistic goals.
- Become impatient with people who do not swiftly and consistently take steps to improve.
- Depend on visible evidence of acceptance and affirmation from others.
- Jump to provide an inspiring answer instead of listening until the other person feels heard.

- Constantly feel the need to be "on" and not let people see you on a bad day.
- Keep people dependent on your positive outlook.

The Lord will use your gift of exhortation to encourage people. The enemy will misuse your gift of exhortation to dishearten people. In the enemy's hands, you will desire to be the one who always brings hope in a dark situation. Taken to extremes, exhorters will dishearten people until others look to you as the ultimate bright spot.

But the Light is God, and He is the One who brings hope in a dark situation.

If you are a *giver* operating from weakness, you may:
- Hoard and hide resources.
- Use gifts and support to control people.
- Become proud of being generous.
- Feel guilty about personal assets.
- Reject all unsolicited appeals for funding.
- Give too sparingly to family.
- Encourage others to look to you rather than to God for provision.
- Wait too long to give in an effort to be sure if a project or person is worthy.
- Harshly judge a person or organization that exhibits poor stewardship.
- Become "too cheap."
- Resent the person or group who comes to you for help too often.
- Make people earn your financial gift.

- Bring up the fact that you gave instead of keeping it a secret.
- Keep people dependent on your financial support.

The Lord will use your gift of giving to support people. The enemy will misuse your gift of giving to lord it over people. In the enemy's hands, you will desire to be the one who always comes through to meet a need. Taken to extremes, givers lord their gifts over people until others look to you as the ultimate provider.

But the Provider is God, and He is the One who comes through to meet every need.

If you are an *organizer* operating from weakness, you may:
- Take charge before being asked.
- Try to build loyalty with favoritism.
- Use people as resources.
- Delegate to avoid work yourself.
- Abuse authority and ignore appeals from those under you.
- Consider the project more important than the people working on it.
- Not confront someone in the wrong because he or she is a valuable asset to your project.
- Be so efficient that no time is taken for explanation or praise.
- Force decisions on others.
- Frustrate others who do not share your vision.
- Keep your plans and real intentions a secret.
- Make followers instead of making leaders.
- Ensure that people wait upon you in order to act.
- Keep people dependent on your direction.

The Lord will use your gift of organizing to motivate people. The enemy will misuse your gift of organizing to demoralize people. In the enemy's hands, you will desire to be the forerunner, the one whom people always follow. Taken to extremes, organizers will demoralize people until others look to you as the ultimate leader.

But the Leader is God, and He is the One we follow.

If you are a *mercy giver* operating from weakness, you may:

- Carry grudges for another person who has been hurt.
- Become possessive of close friendships.
- Be tolerant of "lesser forms" of sin.
- Not confront someone in the wrong because you feel pity for them.
- Avoid discipline and conflict.
- Base important decisions on emotions alone.
- Accidentally cross lines with members of the opposite sex as you show compassion and empathy.
- Feel bitter toward God when good people are allowed to suffer.
- Cut off insensitive people.
- Allow others to become reliant upon you for comfort so that they do not move on.
- Rescue people who do not need to be rescued.
- Fail to set boundaries for someone you feel sorry for.
- Feel offended when others do not show what you think is proper compassion for you, cultivating a victim mentality.
- Keep people dependent on your emotional support.

The Lord will use your gift of mercy to strengthen hurting people. The enemy will misuse your gift of mercy to incapacitate people. In the enemy's hands, you will desire to be the one who always understands. Taken to extremes, mercy givers will incapacitate people until they look to you as the ultimate comfort.

But the Comforter is God, and He is the One who always understands.

Many people may have come to mind as we walked through those lists of misused gifts. My deepest desire is that you will begin to see these people with fresh insight. Please recognize that the quality that repulses you in another person might be what God meant to be their gift to the Kingdom . . . but the enemy has hijacked it temporarily. Perhaps this realization will enliven and redirect your prayers for those around you.

And just in case you would like some clarity, I have a personal example, my friends.

My motivational gift is exhortation. I am born to encourage. There is nothing I love more than pointing people toward hope. Trials can be almost thrilling for me because, by now, I have come to look forward to a great move of God within every struggle. It is easy for me to have faith, and it is easy for me to inspire faith in others. That is the whole idea of a spiritual gift, you see. It is easy for me to give exhortation, not because I am so good at producing it, but because I already have it on hand. I have been given that gift to give. The exhortation in me came to me at no cost. There is an endless supply of it as long as I rest and abide in Jesus so that I am filled with the fruit of the Spirit. I will never run out of it for myself and to give away to others. I can write as many encouraging books as time will allow. I can give as many encouraging messages as my voice will allow. If I stay close enough to hear God's heartbeat, I simply won't run out of hope-giving words for the church and for the world. That is the supernatural mechanism of a spiritual gift.

When you are abiding in Christ, the gift works, you don't.

Several years ago, I bought my first house and had a joyful time decorating every inch of it. A few years passed, and I realized that I had only invited a handful of people over. That had not been my intention. When I purchased the property, I meant to have dozens of people over every few months. Serving is *not* my go-to gift, however. Even when I am a guest at a dinner party, I can't figure out what I should do to help. My mind spins. I don't know what to do with my hands.

I say to myself, *What should I do? Make the salad? Mine are never very good-looking. Should I bring the meal to the table? I can't walk with a heavy dish without tripping. Should I put ice in the glasses? Is it too soon? Oh, why can't I just sit on a barstool and tell the cook that what they are creating smells wonderful, looks lovely, and they are doing a fantastic job?*

Do you see what happened there? I would rather encourage the cook than serve with him. Even when I try to function as a server, I automatically revert to functioning as an exhorter because that is my design. Now it makes me smile to see the pattern in myself. I finally get it. Trust me, you don't want my casseroles as much as you want my encouragement notes. Yet, for many years, I thought the fact that I didn't find it easy to serve was a character flaw in me as a woman. I wanted to be good at the things *I* wanted to be good at; I wanted to do the things that I thought made me look good or that other people appreciated more. Instead of flowing in the capacities that God has created in me, I tried to re-create myself. Instead of relying on love, joy, peace, patience, kindness, goodness, gentleness, faithfulness, and self-control . . . I relied on myself.

I decided that I really *was* a server who just needed more opportunities to exercise my serving skills. I read books about entertaining guests and decided to invite a group of seven women over to my house, every Tuesday for nine weeks. Does the thought of it make your neck tense immediately? Right off the bat I invited, not just one or two friends over for dinner, but *seven*—a full-blown dinner party. And I planned to host, not just one dinner party, but nine in a row—a full-blown fantasy. Now before I tell you the next fact, which will really make you question my sanity, I want to tell you that we will always revert to our God-given design, even when we try to resist it. What you will see unfolding in this story is not an exhorter transforming into a strong server, but an exhorter operating as a weak exhorter. Remember the core quality of an exhorter: we don't quit. Exhorters keep going. We thrive in a challenging situation and see it as an opportunity for spiritual growth and increased faith. We *assume* things will be hard. Hardships give us a chance to dig deeper and abide closer.

The phenomenon is that when exhorters begin to operate from weakness, they can accidentally *produce their own challenges* through which they can persevere! Sometimes I am blind to the ways that I invent unnecessary difficulties for myself.

As soon as I received the RSVPs from the seven friends who would be coming over to my house for dinner parties nine Tuesdays in a row, I decided that this serving thing was going to work! The transformation had begun! So I sent out *more* invitations. Why not? The only thing better than one dinner party every week is . . . TWO!

Within a few days, I had seven more RSVPs from friends who would be coming to my house for dinner parties on nine *Mondays* in a row. I was going to have eighteen dinner parties in less than three months! Hoorah!

Never mind that I had not had so much as eighteen *individual people* over in the last three *years*.

Never mind that I did not even own a dining room table.

Or chairs.

I don't even know if a real server would do something like this. They would probably know better. But an exhorter who is trying very hard to be a server? This was a golden opportunity for faith. You don't have a table? Ask God for a table! He will provide! You don't have chairs? Go ahead and invite the people, and rely on God to make sure they have a place to sit! I started praying fervently for a table and chairs. I moved the desk and other office supplies out of my dining room in expectancy. The only thing I left in the room was the Oriental rug and my mother's china hutch, which did not hold dishes. I had filled it with faith books and Bibles and used it as a bookcase.

Which is exactly what an exhorter would do with a china hutch, right?

I considered buying a dining set at a garage sale or a thrift store but felt the Lord asking me to wait. So I prayed more. I did not mention my need to anyone. I prayed over my empty dining room every day and waited. I leaned into God. And then one week before my first two dinner parties, I received a random message from someone I had not talked to in a long time. She wanted to know if I wanted a dining room table and chairs. For free. She was about to put the set in her garage sale but felt she needed to ask *me* first.

Why?

Because the dining room set had been given to her fifteen years earlier.

By my mother.

This friend was asking if I wanted *the* dining set that my parents had bought when I was in elementary school. It was the set I had grown up with in my childhood home. In fact, I already had the *matching* china hutch. I had completely forgotten that when my brother and I had gone to college, my mother had given the table and chairs to friends who could use them more than she would. She'd kept the hutch.

Yes. Without my saying a word to anyone, I received a sudden opportunity to get my own long-lost childhood table and chairs back *one week before I began a series of eighteen dinner parties.*

You can call that offer what you want to, but I call it a miracle. I again returned to my knees, praying my jubilant thanksgiving to the God who provides. It seemed that His favor and blessing were all over my new capacity as a server in the Kingdom.

Then something else happened the week before the first dinner parties. I stopped praying. Oh, I still prayed some, but not with the same intensity, length, or focus. I interpreted that table as my big green light of glory from the Lord and then started trying to serve in my own power. And it is not like God didn't try to warn me that I was making myself vulnerable. In fact, He warned me explicitly. I was setting that very first dinner table a day or two in advance, and was using a mix-and-match combination of my mother's china and both grandmothers' china. All three coordinated beautifully with their pale-gray patterns. The table was stunning, and I returned to the kitchen smiling. Then I tripped on my own two feet. When I reached out with both hands to catch myself as I plunged forward, my left arm swept the countertop, where I had placed all of the remaining pieces of all three sets of china. I landed on the floor on my back and put my arms up to cover my face. Plates, cups, and platters crashed all around me. When the avalanche stopped, I was breathless, still, silent, and surrounded by broken pieces.

Expect opposition.

God spoke into my heart so clearly, it was as if He were kneeling beside me in the porcelain ruins.

Expect opposition, He said.

At the time, I thought that might mean that the enemy would bring opposition through accidents and troubles, such as tripping and breaking the dishes. What I know now is that the enemy would bring opposition by using me against myself. Over the next three months, I experienced a wonderful time of fellowship with my friends at each of the eighteen dinner parties, but I wore myself out. My limited mobility was tested to the utmost. Both knees swelled from so much time spent standing in the kitchen. I was constantly cleaning my house and would collapse in bed each night in fatigue. But because I was operating in my exhorting weakness, I buoyed myself and kept going.

In the wrong direction.

By the time it was over, I was dismayed, and I knew it was my own fault. Thankfully, we tend to learn the most when we are in crisis. During that time, I learned so much about housekeeping, and cooking, and hosting parties. I hope the parties were a pleasure to my guests, but they came at a needless physical price to me. There was no reason for me to jump into the endeavor to that degree. The most important lesson I learned from that experience is that God wants to use our go-to gifts to bless both ourselves and others, and the enemy wants to use them to harm both ourselves and others.

Now, this may sound counterintuitive, but believers tend to think operating in our gifts should be hard work. Maybe we have been trained to think we must labor for the Lord, that a sacrifice should cost us something or be painful. True, a sacrifice is only a sacrifice if it costs us something, but I don't think it costs what we have always thought.

God never asks for the sacrifice of more and harder *work* from us. He asks for the sacrifice of our *lives*. He asks us to surrender our control to Him so that He can re-create our overworked selves into fully productive children of the King of kings.

"My yoke is easy," He said. "My burden is light."[4]

Did you catch that? It's *supposed* to be easy.

We make it hard when we try to operate in a gift without being nourished and strengthened by the fruit of the Spirit. How would this story have been different if I had exercised self-control, choosing to host one or two parties to gain some experience and success before jumping into an overwhelming commitment? How would it have been different if I had taken hold of peace and decided to be content with what I could do safely and effectively, instead of trying to do it all? How would it have looked if I had cultivated kindness, showing it not only to my guests *but to myself*?

Pray for discernment about yourself as you think of my story of trying to be productive for the Lord while relying on my own efforts. When I stepped outside of my basic design, I ceased to abide in Christ. Ask the Holy Spirit to reveal to you the times in your life when you may have done the same thing.

If we want to burst forth with fruitfulness and productivity, then we must entrust our gifts to the Master Gardener, who makes all things grow. Your gifts will increase *along with* the fruit that is necessary to sustain them. To entrust our gifts to Him is to flow in the design of our gifts as He created them in us. Only in that way will we be productive. This does not mean that we are "stuck" in the function of only one gift. By sharing my dinner party story, I did not intend to say that an exhorter can never serve. But I do think that when my acts of service are viewed through my exhortation lens, then I view serving in a healthy way.

What do I mean? I wouldn't have put so much emphasis on

making all the food from scratch and having fresh flowers and a pressed tablecloth and using china every week. In pretending to be a server, I thought I had to make the presentation about what I could do, which is not the way a real server thinks. But if I were throwing a dinner party through an exhorter's lens, I would plan the entire event with the encouragement of my guests in mind. I still love a well-dressed table and flowers, but this time I might order take-out and spend the cooking time thinking of uplifting conversation starters, creating a playlist of cheerful background music, planning after-dinner games, or designing unique place cards with a blessing written for each person. By the time I sat down to the table with my guests, I would be refreshed, not tired, because I had been operating in my exhorter strength as I served.

I would be well-nourished by the fine fruit of goodness, patience, and joy.

I would be abiding in Him.

As you seek new life, you must abide in Christ like never before. You are in a time when you must water the word God has spoken over you by praying, fasting, and meditating on Scripture. Continue this sacred practice by writing these verses in your journal and reading them out loud over yourself. Don't forget to look yourself in the eye between the lines you read.

Let There Be Productivity
(from John 15:1-8)

I know that I, _____, am a branch, created in Christ Jesus. Jesus is the True Vine, and God the Father is the Gardener. He cuts off every branch that bears no fruit, while every branch that does bear fruit He prunes so that it will be even more fruitful. I am already clean because of the word He has spoken to me. I will remain in Him, as He also remains in me. No branch can bear fruit by itself; it must remain in Jesus, the Vine. Neither can I bear fruit unless I remain in Him.

Jesus is the Vine; I am one of the branches. If I remain in Him and He in me, I will bear much fruit; apart from Him I can do nothing. If I do not remain in Him, I am like a branch that is thrown away and withers; such branches are picked up, thrown into the fire, and burned. If I remain in Him and His words remain in me, I can ask whatever I wish, and it will be done for me. This is to the Father's glory, that I bear much fruit, showing myself to be His disciple.

Jesus said, "Live in me. Make your home in me just as I do in you. In the same way that a branch can't bear grapes by itself but only by being joined to the vine, you can't bear fruit unless you are joined with me."[5] We simply will not be fruitful if we do not stay with Him.

But if we do stay with Him?

To those who remain close, He says, "I am the Vine, you are the branches. When you're joined with me and I with you, the relation intimate and organic, the harvest is sure to be abundant."[6]

In other words, the land—we who are made of earth—will burst forth with fruitfulness.

EIGHT

Productivity

THE TRUTH IS, sometimes abiding in Christ means being still, and being still feels unproductive. I am the girl who opens the microwave door when there are five seconds remaining on the timer. I don't want to be still and do nothing.

But meditating can be strengthening stillness.

It is not easy. The most difficult thing to keep still is my mouth. I have to work hard, training myself to let the Holy Spirit's voice speak into a situation instead of my own. If I do not discipline myself to meditate, then I usually default to worrying, which is not only unproductive, it is destructive.

One way I practice meditation is through instrumental praise music. I *listen* without singing the words back into the songs. I *listen* without humming. I *listen* without reading or praying or moving. I just *listen*, being as still as possible, and think about how big God is, about how small my problems really are, and about how He has led me through every battle I've ever faced. It can be healing to meditate on God's sovereignty this way.

Even my physician—who seeks to treat his patients in spirit, soul, *and* body—strongly recommends meditating to worship music for at least ten minutes a day. He says the overall health benefits cannot be overstated.

If you are like me, then you know what a challenge this is. I stray off task every time. I will be meditating, and then catch myself having missed half of the song because my mind wandered to a thousand other things. When that happens, I just try to refocus and continue. My ability to be still has gotten better with practice; that is the good news. Now the gentle notes of the songs pour over me and bathe my heart in peace. By the end I feel secure and strong and revived.

Meditation is one way that I access the fruit of the Spirit.

One day I had experienced just such a time of strengthening stillness, then I went to work at the school where I was teaching fifth grade. It was a routine and uneventful morning. Just before lunch, I received some unsettling news from a colleague. I stood there in the hallway, and all at once, my tranquility crumbled. Fury flashed inside me; I could feel it burning in my face. I gritted my teeth as I walked back into my classroom, only to see twenty-seven pairs of eleven-year-old eyes watching every move I made.

I had an audience. But in my sudden bad mood, I was not about to display what it means to be filled with the fruit of the Spirit. If I had spoken, the tone of my voice would have been telling. My furrowed brow was already communicating enough.

Isn't it interesting that one of the first things we do when we are angry is to make fists? It is almost involuntary. Whenever I became mad as a teenager, I made fists and felt like punching walls or doors . . . and sometimes I did. That day in my classroom, it occurred to me that my hands were balled into angry fists at my sides. Suddenly I decided to do something different with the fists

I had made. I slowly and consciously put one fist over my mouth. I didn't flatten my hand. I left it in a fist on top of my lips to hold them closed, as if I were rolling a stone over a tomb. Trust me, in that moment, my mouth *was* a tomb, because the words I would have spoken, even to mutter under my breath, would not have been life-giving.

A wise friend of mine says that when we are in a crisis, we default to what is familiar. "If you have a history of making poor decisions," she tells me, "a crisis is not the time that the wisest decisions of your life are suddenly going to pour forth. Planning ahead will make the right decisions part of what is familiar to your heart."

If we want to react well when it counts, we have to write a new script for ourselves. We have to practice the text of who we want to be in a crisis.

I saw the benefit of "planning for a new familiar" in my classroom that day. It was time for my students to go to the cafeteria for lunch, just minutes after I had received the infuriating news. With one fist still over my mouth, I used the other hand to wave for the class to line up silently as usual. They were used to our routines without my having to speak instructions, so I walked them to lunch with my fist over my mouth the whole way.

If I had defaulted to what was familiar when I came back from the school cafeteria to my empty classroom, I would have left campus immediately and sped away for my own fast-food lunch. Look, when I've got only twenty-five minutes to feel better, I grab a large Dr Pepper and two burritos. Maybe some chips and queso. If I have a smaller sliver of time, I can become an unstoppable force on the bowl of Hershey's miniatures in the teachers' lounge. This plan has *never* made me feel better, but I've rarely deviated from my personal mantra: "If you can't say something nice, then stuff something in your mouth."

But I had meditated in worship of the Lord that morning, so I had a new plan this time. I would choose to reach through my frustration and access the fruit of the Spirit.

I closed the classroom door, turned out the lights, and reached for my phone. I swiped until I found the instrumental praise music and closed my eyes. Instantly, I felt my blood pressure drop and the heat in my face cool away. It wasn't hard for me to remember everything I had meditated on that morning: God is big, my problems are small, and He's led me through every battle I've ever faced.

Then fruit did something that queso couldn't. It revived my heart.

God will not entrust His precious plan to us until He knows that *we* trust *Him*. If we want to be productive, then defaulting to the fruit of the Spirit has to become the familiar. We need to be practicing the text of who we were meant to be. And, yes, we were meant to bear fruit.

By the time my class came back from lunch, they had a brand-new teacher: me.

And I'm glad. The lessons we teach children rarely happen during "the lesson." Those students sensed my peaceful heart, which wasn't just an attempt to act my way out of how I really felt. God had brought about a genuine shift in my countenance through twenty-five minutes of silent surrender at my desk. I had not prayed a specific prayer. In fact, I had not prayed at all. I had only focused on being still and listening to praise music, music that reminds me of who He is. I had invited God in instead of shutting Him out with my own solutions. Letting His presence fill the room was enough to make my critical issue seem like nothing beside Him.

That's what I keep forgetting: my problems are nothing for Him to fix. I don't have to try to solve everything, I just need to sit in strengthening stillness and let Him do it.

Whenever I am about to lose focus or patience, I coach myself to think of Exodus 14:14.

First, I need to think of it in the New International Version, where it says so clearly, "The LORD will fight for you; *you need only to be still*" (emphasis mine).

And then I need to think of it in the New King James Version: "The LORD will fight for you, and *you shall hold your peace*" (emphasis mine).

And then I need to think of it in the New Living Translation: "The LORD himself will fight for you. *Just stay calm*" (emphasis mine).

And then I need to think of it in *The Message*: "GOD will fight the battle for you. *And you? You keep your mouths shut!*" (emphasis mine).

Be still.

Hold your peace.

Stay calm.

Keep your mouth shut.

Okay, okay, I get it. God is going to fight my battles for me. But God starts to fight when the timing is right, and sometimes it is hard to wait on Him.

Enter *patience*: that pesky fruit of the Spirit that brings kings to their knees.

In the Bible, young David exercises princely patience, waiting years and years to see God move in a big way and make him king. During the wait, he must have felt he was in the pit of non-productivity.

While he waits, he thinks back to the day that Samuel prayed, and the royal promise poured over David's windblown hair. Anointing oil pooled in his open palms.

Maybe he asked, "When? *When* will it happen?"

"Not yet. Not today," I can hear wise old Samuel answer. This is not the boy he would have picked in the first place. He had expected someone more mature, someone like the other brothers. He pauses, thinking how young he was when the Lord called him. Samuel sighs. *Yahweh's thoughts are not our thoughts.* He cannot begin to predict *when* David's kingship will begin.

The prophet and the shepherd both go back to work.

Maybe the mud looks deeper to David; maybe the sheep smell worse; maybe the sun seems hotter after he hears the first hint of his destiny. Maybe the workdays feel longer. Maybe there is too much time to think and too much lonely shepherd silence. Sheep manure and craggy rocks can do something to a man who is waiting for a crown.

But suddenly things are looking up!

David becomes a musician in the palace courts. Surely he is getting closer to the dream; he is actually *in the palace* now. In the palace! This must be it! Later, he is victorious over Goliath, and his name and the word *king* are mentioned together once again, this time by citizens chanting the praises of King Saul *and* David as they ride through Jerusalem. He goes from a crowd of animals to a crowd of admirers, and anyone would bet he is close to the throne.

He is not on his way there just yet. In fact, a little bit later, he is on his way *out* of the city. Fast and on foot.

David must wonder what happened to the promise in the field. Now that King Saul has put a price on his head, David probably looks back on his old farm life with fondness. During the long, insomniac nights as a hunted man, he isn't just counting sheep. He is wishing he was back home with them. However, there are certain steps of obedience that prevent us from turning back, and David has taken too many of them. He can't go home. His only choices are to keep believing in his destiny, give up on it, or get mad about it. He chooses to keep believing, but even that decision is peppered with plenty of questions.

> My soul is in deep anguish.
> > How long, Lord, how long?[7]

> Why, Lord, do you stand far off?
> > Why do you hide yourself in times of trouble?[8]

> My God, my God, why have you forsaken me?
> Why are you so far from saving me,
> > so far from my cries of anguish?[9]

David trusts God enough to have a genuine relationship with Him. He doesn't try to hide his thoughts from the One who knows him best. The Psalms are a roller coaster of elation and agony, and they are as real as it gets. David feels helpless when he is running for his life with the royal army in dogged pursuit. He looks to God every evening, every morning, and in the heat of every day. He lifts his eyes to the hills. He is hoping that help from the Lord will soon come running over them.

One day it does. David looks up and sees this:

> These are the numbers of the men armed for battle who came to David at Hebron to turn Saul's kingdom over to him, as the Lord had said:
> > from Judah, carrying shield and spear—6,800 armed for battle;
> > from Simeon, warriors ready for battle—7,100;

from Levi—4,600, including Jehoiada, leader of the family of Aaron, with 3,700 men, and Zadok, a brave young warrior, with 22 officers from his family;

from Benjamin, Saul's tribe—3,000, most of whom had remained loyal to Saul's house until then;

from Ephraim, brave warriors, famous in their own clans—20,800;

from half the tribe of Manasseh, *designated by name to come and make David king*—18,000;

from Issachar, *men who understood the times and knew what Israel should do*—200 chiefs, with all their relatives under their command;

from Zebulun, experienced soldiers prepared for battle with every type of weapon, *to help David with undivided loyalty*—50,000;

from Naphtali—1,000 officers, together with 37,000 men carrying shields and spears;

from Dan, ready for battle—28,600;

from Asher, experienced soldiers prepared for battle—40,000;

and from east of the Jordan, from Reuben, Gad and the half-tribe of Manasseh, armed with every type of weapon—120,000.

All these were fighting men who volunteered to serve in the ranks. *They came to Hebron fully determined to make David king over all Israel. All the rest of the Israelites were also of one mind to make David king.*[10]

Add it up! Add it up!

Can you imagine the thundering volume of that many

warriors as they marched into Hebron in full battle array? The ground must have shaken! And every last one of these men, some of whom are described as having faces "like the faces of lions,"[11] came specifically to escort David into his royal role. They were "fully determined" and "were also of one mind." David doesn't have to wonder if his time has come. He *knows* it has.

The Lord empowers us not a moment too soon.

We don't have to engineer things to get help when it is the right time. We don't have to orchestrate, or worry that we will miss our chance. We can trust Him enough to be still and abide. When the time is right, we will know it because we will see our Deliverer coming over the hills for us.

The only difference between fruit that is hard and green, fruit that is ripe and sweet, and fruit that is bruised and rotten is a delicate timeline. Fruit is living so it has a life span. There is a beginning, middle, and end. That is one thing that many believers do not realize about the fruit of the Spirit. We pray and expect the Lord to just drop love, joy, peace, patience, kindness, goodness, faithful, gentleness, and self-control into our hearts and minds. I have never seen a fruit tree that bore fruit suddenly. There's no such thing as a fruit eruption. A maturation process occurs before there is fruit. And once there is fruit, it is there for the taking, eating, and enjoying.

But the fruit does not exist indefinitely. It is on the branch for a time and season, and then it falls so that the seeds within it are planted and will produce more trees and more fruit. When I acknowledged this process, it helped me understand my own heart.

There are days when a sudden blow knocks me over, like the time in my classroom that I mentioned before. It could be that the discomfort can even be traced back to a specific person. I will be tempted to think that it is their fault for saying or doing something to me. Those are the moments when I find out whether I have been abiding. There will either be fruit of the Holy Spirit for the picking or not. If I cannot reach for peace and patience in a circumstance, then that is a problem I have with the Holy Spirit, not a problem I have with people. If I cannot bring forth love and faithfulness for someone who has hurt me, then that, too, is a Holy Spirit problem, which is ultimately *my* problem, not someone else's. A lack of fruit is *my* problem because the only person who can tend the orchard of my heart is me. So I have learned to plant trees with the persistence of Johnny Appleseed.

Good fruit doesn't grow by chance. It grows when you plant.

Sometimes the fruit I once had is fallen and rotten, and we have to be honest about how many times this has happened for each of us. Hopefully, as we abide, there will be love, joy, peace, patience, kindness, goodness, gentleness, faithfulness, and self-control in our orchards in a constant cycle. The fruit should be there for us to access so we can respond in better ways.

Uncommon fruitfulness, the kind Jesus talks about, has a lot to do with words—*whose* words we use and *how* we use them. Look at how many times He says it:

If you remain in me and my words remain in you, ask whatever you wish, and it will be done for you. This is to my Father's glory, that you bear much fruit, showing yourselves to be my disciples.[12]

You did not choose me, but I chose you and appointed you so that you might go and bear fruit—fruit that will last—and so that whatever you ask in my name the Father will give you.[13]

The tongue has the power of life and death,
and those who love it will eat its fruit.[14]

We must step aside and let the Great Gardener, the Master of Eden, slowly bring about what He desires in our lives. Vegetation needs a chance to grow. While we wait for the right timing, we must be very careful how we use our mouths. When Jesus anointed you for the task He had "prepared in advance for [you] to do,"[15] He was planting a seed. Oh, did you think you were going to see fruit the very next day? What about the roots? What about the trunk or stem? What about the branches? All of that comes first. There is a lot of character training that has to come before Kingdom productivity.

It is important to remember that our great desire to be productive is from the Lord, and it is not selfish. He is productive, and we are made in His image. He will make us more and more like Himself through a training process, and as that happens, the fruit is being formed.

In discussing David's great angst in wondering how and when his anointing would take him from shepherd to king, we can focus on the treasured first line of Psalm 23: "The LORD is my shepherd; I have *all that I need*."[16]

In the New Testament, Peter knew the Shepherd of shepherds too. He writes his own version of the Twenty-Third Psalm: "His divine power has given us *everything we need* for a godly life through our knowledge of him who called us by his own glory and goodness."[17]

We have everything we need to bear fruit. We have Jesus, the Good Shepherd. We must believe His words and not anyone else's. A Good Shepherd "goes on ahead of [His sheep], and his sheep follow him because they know his voice. But they will never follow a stranger; in fact, they will run away from him because they do not recognize a stranger's voice."[18]

Then He says it again: "I am the good shepherd; I know my own sheep, and they know me. . . . They will listen to my voice."[19]

Of course you know *why* He wants us to listen to and follow His voice and not another. It is because God has made the hearts of His children the most fertile fields on Earth. We are full of life. Whatever we bring into ourselves comes to life. Therefore, every spoken word—good or bad—is a seed that is planted in our hearts, everything that is planted in our hearts produces a crop, and we will dine on its harvest. Life and death are in the power of the tongue, and we will eat its fruit! We must be careful about what we say.

What comes out of our mouths eventually goes back into them.

Those who know the Good Shepherd's voice follow His voice. Jesus warns us that His real sheep are recognizable. His sheep know His voice and plant the seed of His words in their hearts, and they will bear a very different harvest from those who listen to a different voice.

Watch out for false prophets. They come to you in sheep's clothing, but inwardly they are ferocious wolves. By their fruit you will recognize them. . . . Every good tree bears good fruit, but a bad tree bears bad fruit. A good tree cannot bear bad fruit, and a bad tree cannot bear good fruit. . . . By their fruit you will recognize them.[20]

You may have known a few wolves who were wearing such high-quality sheep costumes that you were almost fooled. But eventually you can always tell the difference between one who follows the voice of the Good Shepherd and one who follows a different voice. That competing voice could be the enemy. It could be well-meaning, meddling people who consider themselves to be prophets. It could be yourself.

Be still. Put your hand over your mouth and stop talking long enough to listen. You will always be able to discern your Good Shepherd's voice. His voice will lead you to the fruit of the Spirit: love, joy, peace, patience, kindness, goodness, faithfulness, gentleness, and self-control. Are the messages you are hearing causing you to bring forth these virtuous responses? If not, run.

Counterfeit voices may sound similar to Jesus, but there is always a dead giveaway.

Fruit.

The Fourth Day

Then God said, "Let lights appear in the sky to separate
the day from the night. Let them be signs to mark
the seasons, days, and years. Let these lights in the sky
shine down on the earth." And that is what happened.
God made two great lights—the larger one to govern
the day, and the smaller one to govern the night.
He also made the stars. God set these lights in the sky
to light the earth, to govern the day and night,
and to separate the light from the darkness.
And God saw that it was good. And evening passed
and morning came, marking the fourth day.

—

GENESIS 1:14–19 NLT

Jesus measures the vast range of light and sections it into smaller pieces. His voice can fragment rays and break beams. Light that was effusive and indirect fractures into shrapnel in His hands.

Sun burns with fiery fury at His fingertips. He tosses the gaseous sphere into the sky. Here is the giant governor of day.

Moon gleams as pearl in His palm. He exhales and stars scatter like glitter across the galaxy, surrounding the moon. Here is the gentle governor of night.

Just like that, there are months.

Seasons.

Years.

Suddenly there is *time*, and it can be measured by the orbital path of the planet. The position of the earth in relation to the sun determines everything about our lives. It is a hint of the truth: the position of the heart in relation to the Son determines everything about our lives.

"Let lights appear in the sky. . . . Let them be signs," He says.

On Day Four, God illuminates the earth with specific lights to serve as signs of time and direction.

NINE

Let There Be Direction

JESUS HARNESSED LIGHT to guide us. He said the sun and moon were to mark the seasons, days, and years. At the inception of these heavenly bodies, He gave us both a gauge to keep time and a compass to give direction: the sun. The light of the sun tells us when to sleep and when to rise. It rises in the east and sets in the west, and by the faithfulness of its course, we have structure.

The Light of the World guides us through our days the same way. By the faithfulness of His character, we have security. And He is the perfect escort everywhere we go because He has been there before.

Have you ever considered that Jesus can see in the dark? He saw that the earth was formless and empty even before He said, "Let there be light." He could have made human beings with the same ability, but He didn't. His design for us is that we would be dependent on Him for direction.

When I was growing up, there was one stoplight in Wedowee, Alabama. My great-aunts Erma and Era, born in 1900 and 1903 respectively, lived as next-door neighbors in that tiny town for years, separated only by a cornfield and differences of opinion. Even in a small town like Wedowee, they didn't cross paths too often. They weren't avoiding one another; their distinct personalities had just carved out two different paths. They shopped at different grocery stores and worshiped at different churches. Their post office was the same, but there wasn't a choice.

The most revealing evidence of my great-aunts' differences came on my favorite Christmas. When I was seven years old, Aunt Erma, the girly girl, gave me a delicate tea set. She urged me to welcome unexpected situations with warmth and grace. Aunt Era, the tomboy, gave me a toolbox. She hoped that I would respond to unexpected situations with determination and grit. In their own ways, they wanted me to be prepared.

Aunt Erma and Aunt Era did not know it, but they were helping to pack the spiritual suitcase I would carry on every winter journey in my life. Erma's grace and Era's grit were the equipment I would use many years later. Often, I would find myself needing *both* characteristics simultaneously. The grace kept me laughing. The grit kept me going.

My two great-aunts also laid the foundation for my love of the Bible. At Aunt Erma's house, I remember rocking on the platform porch swing after supper, laughing and shelling peas until we could not stop ourselves from yawning. Later, she would tuck us in, reciting the Lord's Prayer and the Twenty-Third Psalm:

"Yea, though I walk through the valley of the shadow of death, I will fear no evil: for thou art with me . . ."[1]

Her sugary Alabama accent was a lullaby, and I always fell asleep before she finished. She held fiercely to the Word of God all her life. There was never a Sunday when she did not fix the Lord's Supper trays for her congregation.

But at Aunt Era's house, I remember following rabbit tracks and spotting snakes in the garden to study later in her books. Aunt Era was the one who taught me to look closely at nature because it was God's precious creation. She also taught me that telling God's stories to children was a special, almost holy, practice. She had a flannelgraph set at home, and I could envision every story she told. It may have been her wrinkles, but at one point, I actually started thinking that she had been a friend of the apostle Paul.

". . . then Saul met Jesus on the road to Damascus, and everything changed. *Everything!* Saul became Paul and turned his whole life around!" she exclaimed, a girlish bloom coming into her cheeks. Paul's story was her favorite. The roadside transformation of an executioner was a thrilling story to tell.

She told of Paul's conversion and read his passionate spiritual letters to us many times. It was not until I was an adult that I learned the stories were real to her because *she* had turned her whole life around too.

Aunt Era was drawn to God quite late in life, after early years of arrogantly rejecting Him. She had lived the first half of her life in wild irreverence. But after she truly came to know her Savior, she changed. Her heart ignited into flame for Him. By the time of her death, she had a stunning two thousand students in Nigeria with whom she conducted one-on-one correspondence courses through World Bible School. Many of those students accepted the Lord and were baptized. She was a global missionary without ever leaving her small, brick house covered by creeping Alabama kudzu. She always dreamed of traveling from Wedowee to western Africa to meet her students, but she never did.

Aunt Era forever will be one of my heroines because she remained approachable. She never let herself get out of humanity's reach. She wasn't ashamed of the mistakes she had made along the way; she didn't hide them. But she wasn't stalled by them either. She had climbed the spiritual heights, had taken in the vista, and then had run down the mountain to get everybody else. She became a travel guide of sorts, and her goal was that every person would find his or her way to Christ.

Some of us take great pains *never* to make a mistake. We think we should show the world how good we are at following Jesus, looking down from the *top* of an isolated spirituality and hollering down, "Come on up!"

But Aunt Era knew better. She had learned she needed to come back down and walk alongside a person, pointing to the pinnacle of faith from the bottom of the mountain and whispering, "I can show you how to get *there*."

Jesus leads us the same way. He will never take us on a path He has not walked Himself. He doesn't holler down from a hill. He stays beside each one of us. Since He has come so far down to meet us, there is no way He would let us advance into the unknown without guidance.

Picture those maps at the shopping mall with a big red arrow, reading, "You are here."

We have received revelation, found freedom, pursued purpose, and practiced productivity. Now we are ready, and we can finally get guidance.

When the Israelites wandered in the wilderness, they needed direction for every step too, and God stayed with them. He showed Himself as a cloud to lead them through the day and as a pillar of fire to lead them through the night. It *is* possible to see clouds at night, you know. Jehovah could have stayed visible in a regular ol' cloud at both times of day. Instead, He chose to intensify His guidance in the dark. He set the cloud aflame. I believe He does the same with us. The darkness only offers us a chance to experience His presence and His direction more intensely than we would otherwise.

And just like He used the different forms of the pillar of cloud and fire, He uses different forms to guide us today. If we desire to follow His *direction*, we must also be willing to follow His *correction*. When I think of this, I cannot help but think about an unfortunate misstep that I witnessed firsthand. So often we learn from seeing events that we never want to repeat.

My mother and I were heading to the restroom during an intermission at Bass Hall, a glorious theater for the arts in downtown Fort Worth. The restrooms are in the lowest level of the hall, down a long marble staircase. Navigating stairs is a challenge for me anyway, but in a long dress and on marble flooring, I needed all the help I could get. I was clinging to the bannister with my right hand and holding fiercely to my mother's arm with my left. We were taking up quite a bit of space as we made our way down the staircase. I heard a few voices behind us that sounded irritated.

"What is taking so long?" a young woman whispered to her date.

After a few more hushed comments from her, she finally erupted a little louder, "This is taking forever! Let's just go around them!"

She must have let go of the railing or his arm, and then she surged forward and squeezed around my mother and me on the left. She was almost in front of us when her high-heeled foot twisted on the second to last step and she lost her balance. Even when her date reached out to catch her, he could not stop the inevitable. My mother and I stared in shock as we witnessed what must be this young woman's "Most Embarrassing Moment" told at every party ever after. Or it could be the story she *never* tells.

Because she couldn't be patient, she took a misstep and fell, her little black dress flying over her head as she went. Then, before her date got to her side and flipped her skirt back in place, all twenty or so people on the staircase could see the large yellow daisies on her white underwear.

I can't help but imagine they drove home in awkward silence that night. I can hear her thinking, *Why couldn't I have waited two more steps—just two more steps?*

But no. She had to step out on her own.

Haven't I done the same thing too many times?

Proverbs 16:18 (MSG) warns us, "First pride, then the crash— the bigger the ego, the harder the fall."

There have been many a "marble staircase" in my life, those situations that require extra caution to navigate. However, caution takes time, and I don't always want to give it. God urges, "Put Me first. Let Me lead. Stay behind Me, and you will be fine."

Again and again, I have become impatient with His pace and stepped out on my own. In each instance, there was a fall of varying degrees. Sometimes it was a huge predicament that I had to get out of, and sometimes it was a moment of intense regret. But every time there was a feeling that I wish I had waited.

This is God's tender and uncomfortable correction, and He permits it—even sends it—because He loves us and wants us to learn to listen. Through correction, He tunes our ears to His voice of guidance, and we become better followers.

The primary way God leads us is through His Word, and there are plenty of places within it where He warns us to stay with Him. If we ever wonder why we are not experiencing His leading, it may be because we have gone off on our own. Isaiah 42:16–20 tells us that failure to listen is the problem:

> I will lead the blind by ways they have not known,
>> along unfamiliar paths I will guide them;
> I will turn the darkness into light before them
>> and make the rough places smooth.
> These are the things I will do;
>> I will not forsake them.
> But those who trust in idols,
>> who say to images, "You are our gods,"
>> will be turned back in utter shame.

> Hear, you deaf;
>> look, you blind, and see!
> Who is blind but my servant,
>> and deaf like the messenger I send?
> Who is blind like the one in covenant with me,
>> blind like the servant of the LORD?
> You have seen many things, but you pay no attention;
>> your ears are open, but you do not listen.

The truth is that maybe we do not hear His guidance because we do not pay attention to it. The last time I was staying in a cabin in the country, I was amazed by the constant birdsong. It thrilled me to hear their cheery tunes as I sat on the porch with my coffee. I couldn't remember how long it had been since I had paid attention to the birds that sing on my own street. When I got back home, I listened intentionally, and I was pleasantly surprised. There was not a difference in the number of birds out in the country versus those in my hometown. The only difference was my level of attention to them. Birds are singing on my street every day, just as loudly as they are in the country. They are never silent. But I only heard them when I gave them audience.

God is speaking through His Word every day. But we only hear Him when we give Him audience.

Sometimes we beg God for clear guidance, waiting for His whispered word, when He has already offered help to us via His written Word. If we refuse to hear Him through *that* line of communication, why do we expect Him to offer another one? I have found that during times when I am desperately needing His direction and do not sense His leading, the thing to do is press into the written Word. I will get up earlier to read or stay up later to read or hunt for scriptures that are specific to my area of concern. I will post these all around my house: writing them with dry-erase markers on my bathroom mirror, tacking them to the bulletin board in the kitchen, sticking them on notes on my car's visor. Sometimes it happens immediately and sometimes it happens over time, but I eventually will know the steps to take. This process may be what James 1:4 (NKJV) means when it implores us to "let patience have its perfect work, that you may be perfect and complete, lacking nothing." We need the wait because the wait leads us to seek answers we already have available.

The Lord promises, "You will seek me and find me when you seek me with all your heart."[2] He isn't saying, if we seek Him, He will come. He is saying, if we seek Him, we will find that He's been there all along. We are already "filled with the full measure of God."[3]

Often, I have heard well-meaning Christians say that "Jesus showed up" in a given situation. The truth is, He's ever present. Jesus isn't the One who needs to show up. We are.

People also speak of "calling down the presence of God"

during worship assemblies. Didn't God say, "I will put my Temple among them forever"?[4] He's not leaving or hiding. We need to be calling *ourselves* to come out of hiding when we begin to worship, not Him.

You may have heard Psalm 22:3 quoted in a worship service from the King James Version: God "inhabitest the praises" of His people. But if we say that too often, we start to miss what it is really explaining, better understood in a modern translation such as the New International Version: God is "enthroned" on the "praises" of His people. He doesn't live in praise. He lives in *us*.[5] Our worship or lack thereof does not determine where He lives. It determines what kind of seat He's invited to take. In our selfish moments we hand Him a folding chair.

When we worship, we offer Him a throne.

Some people even believe they should be "praying up" before they take on an act of ministry. We don't pray in order to get Him to empower us when and where we need it. We pray because He has already filled us with power, and we are acknowledging where it comes from.

Now I fully believe that "His divine power has given us everything we need for a godly life."[6] I have finally learned to stop sitting idly where I am, expecting God to speak something new to me. Instead, I have started paying attention to what He is already saying. And not *just* paying attention to Him, but applying everything He's said with everything I've got. James 1:21-25 (NIV) exhorts us to:

> Humbly accept the word planted in you, which can save you. Do not merely listen to the word, and so deceive yourselves. Do what it says. Anyone who listens to the word but does not do what it says is like someone who

looks at his face in a mirror and, after looking at himself, goes away and immediately forgets what he looks like. But whoever looks intently into the perfect law that gives freedom, and continues in it—not forgetting what they have heard, but doing it—they will be blessed in what they do.

Too many times, I have looked in the mirror and walked away with amnesia, forgetting what I already have. I want to accept the Word planted in me and examine each day for a trace of His steps, remembering that He has gone before me in all things. His guidance will be His footprints.

The next declaration we must make in our journals and out loud is to embrace the truth that we do not have to beg God for His guidance or coerce Him to "show up" or prepare ourselves by "praying up." He is already here and has already gone before us, and we are already prepared.

Let There Be Guidance
(from Psalm 139 NLT)

I, _____, know, O Lord, that You have examined my heart and know everything about me. You know when I sit down or stand up. You know my thoughts even when I'm far away. You see me when I travel and when I rest at home. You know everything I do. You know what I am going to say even before I say it, Lord. You go before me and follow me. You place your hand of blessing on my head. Such knowledge is too wonderful for me, too great for me to understand!

I can never escape from Your Spirit! I can never get away from Your presence! If I go up to heaven, You are there; if I go down to the grave, You are there. If I ride the wings of the morning, if I dwell by the farthest oceans, even there Your hand will guide me, and Your strength will support me. I could ask the darkness to hide me and the light around me to become night—but even in darkness I cannot hide from You. To You the night shines as bright as day. Darkness and light are the same to You. . . .

You saw me before I was born. Every day of my life was recorded in Your book. Every moment was laid out before a single day had passed.

How precious are Your thoughts about me, O God. They cannot be numbered! I can't even count them; they outnumber the grains of sand! And when I wake up, You are still with me! . . .

Search me, O God, and know my heart; test me and know my anxious thoughts. Point out anything in me that offends You, and lead me along the path of everlasting life.

Maybe if we start listening to Him, we'll discover He has a lot to say. Maybe if we start following Him, we'll discover He has established the way.

You can expect to be blessed if you put Him first and then follow.

God honors His pursuers.

TEN

Guidance

MY INTENTIONAL SOLITUDE occurs in the early morning hours. This is when I hear God, when I pursue His guidance. The confusion melts away.

I finally admitted that I can cultivate solitude best in the morning. Some people can craft quiet time as they are going to bed at night, but I cannot. I just fall asleep. (Hey, being with God can be peaceful.) Besides, someone once reminded me that if orchestras intend to play well, they warm up *before* the symphony, not *after*. That musical metaphor resonates in my heart. Seeking God in the morning makes more sense if we intend to "play the day" with any grace. Yet even in the morning, I face obstacles. And perhaps in the morning they are more abundant.

The day has started, so I want to see what has happened on my e-mail and social feeds overnight. I have lists to make: the groceries I will buy, the errands I will run, the people I will call when the sun comes up. I have a calendar to consult. The newborn day is less than an hour old, and already it has grown quite big and loud. But to encounter God in a meaningful way, I know I must make myself small and silent. I must be focused. So the timer on my watch is my tiny coach. This timer has made all the difference. I set it and then let go of mindfulness and concern. I can close my eyes, making the commitment not to look anywhere else but into His face. No checking the clock. No scanning my calendar or messages.

First, Him.

It has taken me a while to get to this point. I remember on my eighteenth birthday I felt that it was time for me to take ownership of my spiritual growth. But there was a problem: I had no idea what I was supposed to do. I asked everyone I admired, "How do you spend your 'quiet time'? What is 'quiet time' supposed to look like?" No one gave me the specific answer I wanted. Maybe that is because it looks different for everyone, and they didn't want to suggest there is only *one* way to approach God. His relationships with people are unique, much like my relationships with people are. With some friends, I share meaningful conversations over coffee on the back porch. With others, I laugh on a road trip or while thrift shopping. With others, we enjoy being together while sewing a project. The art of connecting is different with each friend I have.

I spent many years attempting and failing my way through various ways of spending time with God. Nothing was consistent. I would begin, but always give up for long periods. Then I would resume later, pulling myself out of a bog of guilt in order to get started. I often quit because my quiet time was not giving me the sense of refreshment I craved. I was too busy flipping back and forth from verse to verse and filling in blanks in a study workbook. It felt like a chore. Yes, the few studies I have finished have been life changing for me. But do you know how many *unfinished* fill-in-the-blank Bible study workbooks languish on my shelf? If workbooks were bricks, I could build a spare room onto your house.

Bible study workbooks are not for everybody. It was a long time before I found a groove that fit *me* and allowed for consistency. I wish I had found it earlier. You might relate to my practice, so I will tell you what I do. This is *not the only way* to pursue time with God, though.

To begin, *I praise.* I sing along with two or three worship songs. You can call me crazy if you want to, but if I am in a hotel or somewhere I can't sing out loud, I will whisper-sing or lip-sync the words. Praise is praise, no matter the volume. Incidentally, I don't play music from a playlist that I have chosen. I use one of the many free web radio services and pull up a station set to praise music. Then I ask God to play three songs that He would like me to sing back to Him that day. He'll do that, you know. Psalm 37:23 says, "The LORD directs the steps of the godly. He delights in *every detail* of their lives" (NLT, emphasis mine). Knowing that He picked the songs that He wanted to hear makes my worship time very personal. It sets the tone for my moments with God and establishes the fact that He is leading it. Sometimes I don't even sing; I read aloud a passage from Psalms that declares His power and might. Remember, God is "enthroned" on the "praises" of His people.[7] Taking the time to praise Him is like pulling up a chair for Him to sit with me. Praise is inviting Him in.

Next, *I engage* with the Bible. I ask the Lord to reveal one sentence of Scripture that I can meditate on throughout the day. I ask Him to meet my needs through His Word. While I read through that day's section of the New Living Translation of the *One Year Bible*, I jump in wholeheartedly.[8] I like the variety of reading the Old Testament, New Testament, Psalms, and Proverbs every day, presented in three to four pages at a time. I underline, highlight, circle words, and write questions in the margins as I read. This is one way of activating my attention and staying alert. I have a better chance of remembering what I have read if I comb my fingers through the information on the page. Think *being in a sandbox* versus *being in a museum*. We have to get involved on a "sandbox level" with the Bible. We're not just there to look; we're there to reach deep into it. You can leave a museum and no one can tell you've been there, but sand stays with you all day, doesn't it? You brush it off, but keep finding grains in the cuff of your shorts or in your shoe. When we leave the Word, we want it to stay with us; we want to be dusted from head to toe with Truth. So what am I digging into the page to find?

I am looking for a personal message from the Lord to guide me through my day.

When I ask the Lord for a personal message of guidance, He always gives me one, and a sentence or two from the Bible will uncannily match my current needs. In my journal, I walk through this sequence:

1. I **copy** the verse, word for word.
2. I **paraphrase** the verse, thinking, *What is the Holy Spirit saying to* any *Christian here?*
3. I **apply** the verse, thinking, *What is the Holy Spirit saying to* me *here?*

This practice began for me when I came across the Discovery Bible Study method, which is more thorough and is an excellent tool to use in small groups, but my ultrasimple version is perfect for my individual Bible reading. All I need to do it is a Bible and a blank journal. I am often tempted to skip the brief life application in step three, but I don't. Taking a moment to apply the Word to my current situation through one written sentence or paragraph is important. In this way, I am engaged; I'm involved, and not just observing. If I do not put the Word into the context of my daily life, I have left the treasure in the chest. And please notice that I do not ask, "What does this verse mean to me?" which leaves *me* as the interpreter of the scripture. No, I ask, "What is the Holy Spirit saying to me here?" because I need to remember that God is the only interpreter of Scripture.

Last, *I pray*, and if I have trouble with distraction or feeling awake and aware, I get on my knees to do it. My mind better focuses on a task when my entire body is also part of the task.

Praise. Engage. Pray. Those are the three steps I take to pursue God's heart. I do this on *most* days. But sometimes I praise the entire time. Or I only engage with the reading, or I only pray. The routine of doing all three helps me, but I am not tied to it.

By the time my watch alarm sounds an hour later, I am ready to continue my morning in the best possible way, washed up and prepared, both inside and out. Ideally, only then will I look at my phone to connect with the specifics of my day. I usually find that I didn't miss anything. If I look at my phone first, and there are plenty of times when I do, I have forfeited the firstfruits that belong to God. Time will become a tide, and I will be swept away with it. Two minutes of browsing on social media will turn into thirty-five; it doesn't matter how disciplined I tell myself I will be. The truth is, if I am disciplined, I will resist from the beginning. All of it can wait, but I have to *make* it wait.

Somewhere a mother is reading this and thinking, *You cannot make children wait.* Friend, be gentle with me. I have not had children yet. But I have taught more than a thousand children in schools. And I believe that they can stand to wait a good deal more than we think. The problem is that we ask them to wait too often when it is insignificant ("Please wait one more minute, I have to finish this text real quick!") and not often enough when it is significant ("Please wait one more minute, I am talking to God right now").

Consider the Herculean example set by Susanna Wesley. Though she gave birth to nineteen children (tragically, nine of them died as infants) and lived in a painfully small home, she found time for solitude in the only way she could: by sitting in a chair and pulling her apron over her head.[9] The Wesley children were well instructed. If Mother has an apron over her head, she is talking to God, and we dare not interrupt. An apron over the head is extreme. And I recognize that it may take gymnastic efforts on your part, too, but just think of the impact of the example you will set. Two of her sons, Charles and John Wesley, went on to become influential in the birth of the Methodist Church. They had learned the importance of intentional solitude because their mother had illustrated it. In fact, their mother had *insisted* upon it.

How long should intentional solitude last? When I tell you this, again, I ask you to be patient with me. I know, I know. I do not have children yet. But I will get to a variation that may fit you if you keep reading.

My quiet time lasts around forty-eight minutes because recently it struck me that God might want us to tithe *everything* He's given us, not just money. What if we gave ten percent of *every* resource, including the valuable commodity of time? Most of us ask God to bless our work. Well, ten percent of our standard eight-hour workday is forty-eight minutes. At the very least, we can give our Creator just forty-eight minutes before we go to do the work we are asking Him to bless.

Forty-eight minutes is a reasonable amount of time for almost everyone. How do I know? Because it is the length of one television show. And one-third the length of an NFL football game. Yes, a televised football game lasts three hours and twelve minutes. If we can make time for a sitcom or sports, then we can make time for anything we prize. Entertainment may relax us, but it does not renew and restore us. Forty-eight minutes with God does. So I shoot for it most days. There are some days it doesn't happen. But I quickly come back to this practice. I know He will bless me if I tithe my time, especially on the busiest days, when I do not think I have that time to set aside. Ninety percent of a day *with* God's guidance is more productive than one hundred percent of a day *without* it.

Now, do I think God would be pleased and honored if I turned this practice of tithing my time into a legalistic expectation? Certainly not. It is only a helpful guideline for me to develop a healthy habit. But habits for habits' sake can be more dangerous than having no habits at all. Oswald Chambers likened it to idolatry:

> Your god may be your little Christian habit, the habit of prayer at stated times, or the habit of Bible reading. Watch how your Father will upset those times if you begin to worship your habit instead of what the habit symbolizes—"I can't do that just now, I am praying; it is my hour with God." No, it is your hour with your habit.[10]

Heaven forbid we feel pride for the way we write the love letter instead of feeling passion for the One to whom we are writing it.

If you would like to grow in the daily practice of connecting with God, and you have not been successful with quiet time before, then do what I did when I was struggling at first: I set my timer for fifteen minutes a day. I praised for five minutes, engaged for five, and prayed for five. It was the starting point I needed. On a hectic day, this fifteen-minute lifeline is still what I use. Fifteen minutes changes the whole day.

I stick with this routine because I want to grow. It feels good to express my anger and frustration and worry, leaving it at His feet. I like being reminded that the One I serve controls the universe. Throughout the day I apply truths I read that morning. His wisdom always recirculates when I need it. I will see a verse, hear a song, have a conversation, and be surprised by the "coincidence" that I had read along that very theme earlier in the day. The Holy Spirit enriches me this way. He knows what I need and when I need it. It is important to remember that He cannot call the wisdom and comfort and guidance of Scripture to the forefront of our minds if there is none in there to begin with.

Internalize the Word *before* you need it, so that you will always have it when you do.

Treasuring up the Word in your heart is not that much different from keeping a little cash on you when you travel. The more money you have on your person—not in a bank account, not in a drawer at home, not in savings bonds, not in stocks, but within immediate reach—the more prepared you are in case of an emergency.

I saw this principle in action when I was moving overseas for an extended mission trip. I had packed numerous books and other supplies, so after I had waited in the slow-grinding line at the airport check-in, I found out my bags were a bit beyond the weight limit. I was not prepared for this because I had weighed them at home and thought all was well. The airline agent told me I would have to pay a difference of $200, and she could only take cash. As I started looking around for the nearest ATM machine, I realized that I would have to get out of the line, get the money, and then come back to the end of the line. I might not make my flight with such a delay. Anxiety seized my heart.

Then a well-traveled friend who had come to see me off walked over and pulled two one-hundred-dollar bills from his wallet, passing them over the counter to the agent. Just like that, the agent processed my baggage, and I watched the suitcases and boxes ease down the conveyor belt.

"I always bring emergency money when I see someone off for an international flight," he said, smiling, "because you just never know." He had prepared himself for the unexpected that morning, and his preparation blessed me remarkably. I was able to make a flight I might have missed. I boarded the plane with a sense of peace.

This is the picture of how we can prepare ourselves with the Word and then use it as an exchange, trading anxiety for peace, when we need to bless ourselves and bless others. *Cash, currency, tender*—no matter what it is called—is nothing more than "a medium of exchange." The voice of the Lord speaks tenderly, so I like to think of it as *tender*. The more of His tender Word I have in my heart at any given time, the more I am prepared with the currency of comfort to give to others when they are shortchanged. The tender of the Word is more than just a means of guidance for us and others; it prepares the path for other people to walk on too.

The difficulty we encounter, whether we want to heed the written Word of God or hear the whispered word of God, is *obeying* that guidance. Sometimes the guiding word is to move. But sometimes the guiding Word is to wait, and the longer we have to wait, the more we are afraid that we have misheard the word.

Could He have really meant for us to wait this long? we think.

When I was teaching high school, I would notice that even

conscientious students would lose concentration and start looking away, out the window or down at their phones. Instead of repeating, "Pay attention," or "Please focus," I would say, "Here's my face." Every time I would say it, my students were conditioned to snap back from their daydreams, turning their eyes and attention toward me.

God calls *us* back too. If we ask God for direction, He always gives it to us. Sometimes He tells us which direction to *move*, and sometimes He tells us which direction to *turn* so that He has our undivided attention. We tend to look away.

Here's My face, He says.

Moving and waiting, moving and waiting, moving and waiting in succession is a typical pattern we see in God's guidance of His people in Scripture. He led the Israelites through the wilderness before they reached the promised land, and we often picture that their forty-year journey was excruciating because of the constant walking. I think it might have been excruciating because of the constant waiting. They certainly weren't walking all the time. They had to move or stay based on the pillar of God's presence hovering over the tabernacle. Sometimes, if the cloud "stayed over the tabernacle for two days or a month or a year, the Israelites would remain in camp and not set out; but when it lifted, they would set out."[11]

They waited a *year*. Ugh.

Some historians say that they may have waited *many years* at a time in one place. But they did so in tents, without planting gardens for food, without establishing a permanent residence, always going to sleep at night with their bags somewhat packed, staying ready to go if the pillar lifted at dawn. The Israelites lived in a semi-permanent state of wait.

You may have felt the same way. If God is your Shepherd,

there are times when He will make you "lie down in green pastures" and wait. And there are also times when He will guide you "along the right paths," bringing honor to His name, even when you "walk through the darkest valley." If God coordinates a move for you, then know that His "goodness and love will follow" you wherever you go.[12]

But if God orchestrates a wait, then know that the wait is never a waste. We have no threat of "time lost, while we are waiting on God's time."[13] He has reasons for delay we cannot see.

Today I took my two nieces and nephew to the park. We enjoyed the bright fall day for three hours, and during that time I must have postponed their play five or six times.

Once, they were about to ride their scooters across the parking lot, but I said, "Wait. Not yet."

"Why do we have to wait?" they asked. They could not see the truck coming, but I saw it. I was trying to keep them alive.

Another time they were ready to run across a field to a good climbing tree, but I said, "Wait. Don't head that way. Go over there and run by the sidewalk to get to it."

"Why can't we run straight there?" they asked, wanting the shorter path. They could not see the muddy creek in their way from their perspective, but I saw it. I was trying to keep them from a mess.

And then they were getting bread to feed the ducks from the dock, but I said, "Wait! Don't throw your bread yet! Quickly move to the other side of the dock and throw your bread into the water there."

"Why do we have to move where there are no ducks?" they asked. They did not realize they were standing near a trash can and bees were buzzing over their heads, but I saw it. I was trying to keep them from pain.

And I knew that as long as they took the bread, the ducks would follow them wherever they went.

Accept God's guidance if He asks you to wait or redirect or move entirely. Trust that He knows about the trucks, and the mud, and the bees, and the ducks, and He wouldn't ask you to wait unless He had a reason.

Besides, He knows that as long as you take the Bread, goodness and love will follow you wherever you go.

The Fifth Day

Then God said, "Let the waters swarm with fish and other life.
Let the skies be filled with birds of every kind."
So God created great sea creatures and every living thing
that scurries and swarms in the water,
and every sort of bird—each producing offspring
of the same kind. And God saw that it was good.
Then God blessed them, saying, "Be fruitful and multiply.
Let the fish fill the seas, and let the birds multiply
on the earth." And evening passed and morning came,
marking the fifth day.

—

GENESIS 1:20–23 NLT

Beneath the glistening waves, God multiplies creatures of every size, whales with mouths like caverns and tiny carp marked with a pinch of shimmer. He stirs the sea with His finger, spinning out a silver whirlpool of barracudas with centrifugal force. The Creator stretches the skin of a puffer fish, then leaves it limp like a balloon, armed and ready to surprise enemies and delight children. God knots colonies of coral like intricate pink macramé. Forming an oyster, He opens its hinge, layering the precious and patient ingredients that will teach us how to make something valuable from difficulty. He laughs, pulling one, two . . . three . . . five . . . eight legs from the knobby head of an octopus. He unfurls the velvet plume of a betta.

Fish cut through the depths, swimming in God's glory.

Into the open sky, He launches an air force: cardinals and hawks and pelicans and storks. He measures His thumb and makes a hummingbird, listening for its purr from petal to perch. God honors the eagle with a regal brow, with speed in its wings, and with the precise eyes of a hunter. He gives mirth to the trill of a robin, making him the cheerful herald of day. He sews poetry into the notes of an owl, making him the throaty balladeer of night.

Birds sail to the heights, soaring in God's praise.

"Let the waters swarm. . . . Let the skies be filled," He says.

On Day Five, God populates the sea and sky.

ELEVEN

Let There Be Life

IN THE BOOK OF JOB, a biblical account of great tragedy, we are surprised to read that Job tells his friends that if animals could talk, they would share many secrets of God's goodness:

> But ask the animals, and they will teach you,
>   or the birds in the sky, and they will tell you;
> or speak to the earth, and it will teach you,
>   or let the fish in the sea inform you.
> Which of all these does not know
>   that the hand of the LORD has done this?
> In his hand is the life of every creature
>   and the breath of all mankind.[1]

The apostle Paul says the same thing:

[People] know the truth about God because he has made it obvious to them. For ever since the world was created, people have seen the earth and sky. Through everything God made, they can clearly see his invisible qualities—

his eternal power and divine nature. So they have no excuse for not knowing God.[2]

All creation tells of the wonder of God. And once we know it for ourselves, we are to tell of it too. We are the church, and the church is the place where God's goodness echoes in a splendid crescendo for all the world to hear. All too often, Christians are content with the idea of being Christians without being the church. This is not possible.

> Together, we are his house, built on the foundation of the apostles and the prophets. And the cornerstone is Christ Jesus himself. We are carefully joined together in him, becoming a holy temple for the Lord. Through him you Gentiles are also being made part of this dwelling where God lives by his Spirit.[3]

We have learned by now that human effort accomplishes nothing, and that we must rely on the Holy Spirit in order to be re-created. However, many of us have tried, or think we have tried, this approach and failed. This is because we have been leaning solely on the fact that God's Spirit lives within us as individuals. This, indeed, is true. But the verses above emphasize that He dwells in us collectively as well. And we miss so much when we dismiss this truth.

For one thing, there is a greater sense of His presence in the church when the church is actually *being* the church. I have heard people say there is an individual anointing of His presence, and a collective anointing as well. The collective anointing is powerful and clear. That may not make immediate sense to you, but I think this analogy will help. I used to drive a twenty-year-old Honda

CRV that would lock up when the battery ran down, which happened several times. I had to have a four-digit code in order to operate the radio after that. The problem was that I had bought the car used and had never been given a radio code. That meant until I could get to the dealership and prove that I owned the car so that they could reset it, I was without a radio or CD player.

Trying to drive without music is like trying to live without oxygen to me.

So I did what I could: I played music on my iPhone. This was fine in residential areas, but once I got on the highway, it was pointless. The hum of the wheels drowned out the music. I remember one time when I had a few friends in the car, and I was wanting to play a song for them. We got on the highway before it was over, and they could no longer hear it, even though my phone was at maximum volume and was positioned in the cup holder to cause a slight sound increase.

"Forget it!" I said. "It's too bad there isn't a way for all of us to turn on our phones to the exact same song at the exact same time. I bet we could hear it then. You just can't hear one phone when there is so much other noise."

The second I said it, I felt the Lord say that it was a picture of what a collective anointing in the church can be like. God is speaking to individuals at maximum volume, but when the hum of our schedules and responsibilities gets too loud, it drowns Him out. Meeting together with other believers in church is a way for all of us to focus our lives on the exact same song at the exact same time. We hear Him more clearly when we come together in His name.

But we miss more than just the corporate anointing when we miss meeting together as the church. The writer of Hebrews describes the incredible encouragement we Christians offer one another when we refuse to live life alone:

And let us consider how we may spur one another on toward love and good deeds, not giving up meeting together, as some are in the habit of doing, but encouraging one another—and all the more as you see the Day approaching.[4]

God can bring about miraculous life change in you if you are willing to be vulnerable with someone in your church. As we have discussed, sometimes that will look like confession. But other times it will look like opening yourself to receive someone's encouragement to do hard things. A great example of this in my life is my friendship with Candy.

Candy and I were acquaintances at church for about ten years, but we were not close friends at all. I tend to be outgoing at church. Candy was the opposite. At the time, she was quiet to the extreme. She almost didn't have a voice. Recently, she laughed and suggested that we probably had spoken three words to one another over the entire first decade of our acquaintance. I laughed too, joking that we had actually only spoken *one* word *three* times: *hey*.

Then a few years ago, Candy sent me a message through social media because she was in distress. Her husband, a lifelong friend of mine, had left her and their two children. She didn't even know where he was. What she *did* know was that he was using methamphetamine. She was writing to me to ask if I would pray with her. Candy was deeply convicted about fighting for her marriage. She felt God had told her to stand for her husband and pray for his restoration. She needed support in what looked to be a long and painful struggle. A lot of people thought she was crazy and counseled her to quit.

Immediately my heart broke for my friend. I knew he had always been a man of character and commitment, and I was willing to hold the vision of who God designed him to be, to work tirelessly with his wife to win him back for the Kingdom. Candy didn't know where to begin, but she was determined. Really, I didn't know where to begin either, but I was just as determined.

She had messaged me at night, and I said we could meet the next evening. I taught school the following day with our evening meeting on my mind the whole time. When the last bell rang, I started thinking I should bring with me something that would be tangible for Candy to take with her when she left. She was really aching, and it is hard to walk away empty-handed when you are hurting that badly.

I closed the door of my classroom, and right there after school, I prayed. I lay my head on my desk, begging the Lord for help. Then I just started typing. On one page, I listed the things I desperately desired for my friend: conviction, a sense of forgiveness, and a mentor, among other things. I looked up a Bible verse for each item on the list. I might have had a few of them memorized, but most of them I searched out on the Internet. We all have amazing access to the Word these days; there is never an excuse not to apply it to specific situations in our lives. Corresponding scriptures are a click away. I searched, "What does the Bible say about addiction?" and "What does the Bible say about family?" There is nothing as powerful as praying God's own Word back to Him. Nothing. It is my favorite way to pray.

When I finished the list, I opened my magic teacher drawer to look through my personal stash of multicolored paper and pulled out two blue sheets, one for me and one for her. Then I printed the pages and left to meet Candy. Our first conversation was stilted as we, near strangers broached such a sensitive topic. I handed her the blue sheet of paper, and we prayed through the list. It was our initial step as prayer partners.

We continued to meet at least every other week for two years. During more than one crisis point, we talked on the phone or she came over and cried. There were occasions when I saw her undertake incredible acts of grace that would not have been possible without the empowering prayer we persisted in regularly. She did merciful and kind things for her husband that I have never seen *anyone* do in the face of rejection. She never pressured him and in fact hardly ever reached out to him. But when he reached out to her, she relied on Christ to help her see her husband through His eyes, and not through her own. She treated him far better than she *felt* like treating him. She treated him far better than he *deserved* to be treated.

Our partnership had been established for a specific time and a particular purpose. Both the time and the purpose were linked. We were meeting regularly to pray for the restoration of her marriage, and we were going to do it until that happened or until God told Candy to stop waiting. With either outcome, she was determined that the story would be fueled by obedience. Many times she wanted to give up, and only her steadfast decision to obey the Lord kept her going.

One of the most memorable events of our journey was what we call our "Jericho Run." I was taking a nap when she texted me that she wanted to go and pray outside the hotel where her husband was staying and spinning further downward into hell on earth. I woke up just enough to groggily reply.

"Sure, I'll go with you to pray over the hotel. Let's do it like Jericho," I texted back. "We can go pray around it seven days in row and then seven times on the seventh day."

Candy replied that it was a plan, and I fell back asleep. When I woke up an hour later, I sat up with a start. *Did I just tell someone that I would pray every night for a week at a dope motel?* I checked my texts. Sure enough, I had. But by that time, Candy and I had prayed so long that I was all in. She wanted her husband back, and I wanted my friend back. We were willing to storm the gates of heaven and hell in order to see his purpose fulfilled. Everyone has a God-given, Kingdom purpose, and this man's wasn't over.

The following day Candy and I drove to the dope motel. Immediately, I could tell that this place was different from any hotel or motel I had seen before. There were bedsheets tacked up in the windows and people walking around outside as if it were a neighborhood block party. We had no precedent for how to conduct a real-life Jericho Run, so we just parked outside, turned on some praise music, and sang a few songs. While we were doing that, a woman on the first floor opened the motel room window (I didn't know that they opened) and popped off the screen. She crawled outside and smoked a cigarette. Then she crawled back into the motel through the window and pulled the screen back in place behind her. Candy and I looked at each other with wide eyes and shrugged.

I said, "She didn't even use the . . . *door*."

This was a battle, and we were in it to win it. We prayed. And then we drove around the motel once and left.

The second night we did it all again. It was great! There was an energy and expectancy to what we were doing. I felt excited.

The third night we did it all again. It went well. I felt good.

The fourth night it was inconvenient to go to the dope motel at our usual time. Candy and I had scheduling conflicts, so instead of making our run at five thirty or so, we had to go at nine thirty. To a bad part of town. But we did it all again. It was not my favorite night. I felt frustrated.

The fifth night I was sick. I thought about calling Candy to say I couldn't go, but I didn't want her to go by herself, which I knew she would do. I went with very little energy. That night we marveled that there were no cops around, patrolling such a hazardous area. We had never even seen one police car. We did it all again. I felt discouraged.

The sixth night was totally draining. I kept wondering why I had said I would come. We were not seeing any difference in any way. The more we looked at that terrible motel, the more it seemed like a mountain that wasn't going to move. This was not just our sixth night of praying for her marriage; it was our sixth night on top of a year of praying. Even still, we did it all again. I felt almost angry.

Be aware that any of us can start a prayer campaign, but the hardest part will come when you get closer to the end, when you will be tempted to quit.

Don't.

On the seventh day, Candy and I woke up with supernatural joy we couldn't explain. We were blazing into the promised land, and we knew it. That evening we called several other friends and asked them to go to the dope motel and caravan with us. We followed our pattern of praising, praying, and circling the motel. There was something holy in the air. You could feel the presence of God.

We all got outside our cars and circled up on the front lawn of the dope motel. I was the last one out, I confess. I was thinking, *Um, can't God hear the prayers we pray from* inside *our cars?* But I got out and prayed with them. Some of the men who were with us walked over and laid hands on the building. Finally, we were ready to move out for the last run around Jericho.

Candy and I were the first car in the caravan, and I was driving.

We drove around once. People on the top floor of the hotel opened their windows and looked out to see what was going on, even though we hadn't made any noise that would have alerted them that something was up. They craned their necks in every direction. They looked down at us suspiciously. Heavenly trouble was coming. I'm serious, it was something you could feel in the air.

We drove around a second time. We drove around a third time. Shirtless men stood in our way, holding out their arms in protest, shouting, "What are you doing here? What are you driving around for?" We just slowly went around them.

We drove around a fourth time. We drove around a fifth time. More people opened the windows and looked down from the third floor.

We drove around a sixth time. We hadn't seen any law enforcement in the entire week, but suddenly we noticed that there were *seven* patrol cars. *Seven* sets of officers raided the cluster of hotels in that area and started bringing tenants out to the curb with their hands zip-tied behind them. It happened so fast. Candy and I looked at one another with wide eyes.

Then I was fired up.

We paused before I drove around the seventh time. I turned to Candy and shouted, "You ready?!" Then I rolled down the windows and let loose. I played worship music as loud as it would go. I threw my left arm out the window in praise, shouting that we were warring against the forces of evil to bring back a son of the Living God.

In the Bible, Joshua was the military leader who defeated Jericho. I took some liberty and mixed that account with a different story of Israelite victory: Gideon's. Gideon was the military leader who defeated Midian, much later in Jewish history. He was nowhere near the real battle of Jericho, but I like what his men said as they rushed into battle. They yelled, "A sword for the LORD and for Gideon!"[5] I tweaked it just a bit to include my friend. I yelled, "A sword for the Lord and for Landon!" Candy just laughed. Tears were streaming down our faces. We knew we were onto something big. We drove around that final time and left the area with a heady sense of victory.

The next day nothing about her situation was different.

It would be another year before we would see what it looks like when walls fall down in a family. But *we* were changed immediately because something happens when two people lay it all on the line and go after a promise together.

Later, after two years of praying together—and by then, Candy was praying with a growing community of friends as well—her husband began to change in visible ways. He had been changing all along, but we just didn't know it. Eventually, he left the twisted life he had temporarily forged for himself and embraced the one that gave him lasting joy. He returned to a better relationship with the Lord, to a better relationship with his wife, and to better relationships with his kids. All of these were sweeter than he had even known before his departure. He makes no secret of the fact that Candy's dedicated prayer for him was what made restoration possible.

She would say that partnering with other believers was what made the prayer possible.

Candy and I remain close, prayerful friends, though we no longer meet regularly like we did when she was in crisis. That level of intensity reached its intended time and purpose. Her personality and approach to life were so altered by the two years she spent growing closer and closer to the Lord that she now has a "voice" that she had never utilized before. She has become a powerful teacher and encourager of prayer and the Word. She leads groups of women at her church who are pursuing the restoration of broken relationships. Her own rich family life is proof that the wait and the warfare are worth it. A supportive Christian community can facilitate a permanent change in your life like few other things can.

The reason God brings us through revelation, freedom, purpose, productivity, and guidance is to take us to the next spiritual level. Community is the next level. New life never stops with you.

That is why the next step on our journey is to journal and pray aloud over ourselves the following declaration:

Let There Be Community
(from 1 Corinthians 13:1-7 NLT)

I, _____, know, O Lord, that if I could speak all the languages of Earth and of angels, but didn't love others, I would only be a noisy gong or a clanging cymbal. If I had the gift of prophecy, and if I understood all of God's secret plans and possessed all knowledge, and if I had such faith that I could move mountains, but didn't love others, I would be nothing. If I gave everything I have to the poor and even sacrificed my body, I could boast about it; but if I didn't love others, I would have gained nothing.

May it be said of me, _____ is patient and kind. _____ is not jealous, or boastful, or proud, or rude. _____ does not demand his/her own way. _____ is not irritable, and keeps no record of being wronged. _____ does not rejoice about injustice but rejoices whenever the truth wins out. _____ never gives up, never loses faith, is always hopeful, and endures through every circumstance.

God designed Christians to live in connection with one another, to pursue Him together and not alone. Even as we see the way He charged birds and fish to multiply and fill their habitats, we know He asks the same of us. Not only are we called to multiply and fill the earth by making disciples, we are called to care for the disciples around us. God exhorts us to "speak encouraging words to one another. Build up hope so you'll all be together in this, no one left out, no one left behind. I know you're already doing this; just keep on doing it."[6]

Surround yourself with friends who know how to encourage. There will be times when you need to remember who you are and what you are here for. You are going to want someone to remind you. And heaven forbid there comes a day when you take enough wrong turns that you end up in a dope motel of your own making. But if it happens, you are going to want someone to come get you.

TWELVE

Community

THERE WERE SEVEN WOMEN on the marriage panel at the women's conference. Some of them came prepared with anecdotes, some with memorable tips for a healthy marriage, some with lists of things they wish they'd never done or said. The audience laughed and cheered and enjoyed every moment.

One panelist all but silenced the crowd when she spoke. Her voice was barely above a whisper. The facilitator had asked, "And what about you? What is the secret to your happy marriage?"

"I am a student of my husband," she said. "I study his heart. I never assume I know everything there is to know about him. And so I pursue him."

The stillness lasted only a moment, and then the focus returned to the other panelists. But her words stayed with me, even after the conference was over. Perhaps some women in the room thought her decision to be a student of her husband was subservient or passive. But to me, it was the picture of active, deliberate love.

My bachelor's education was mostly a time for fun, but in graduate school, I finally learned the reality of being a student. To study is to esteem. When we study something, we pour our energies in the direction of what we value. We give our time, attention, and exorbitant funds in the pursuit of that thing. In fact, we go into it intending to change. We want to pattern ourselves after that which we pursue.

By saying she was a student of her husband, the woman on the panel was saying that she was so motivated by love and she so esteemed her husband's heart that she poured her energies into the study of it in order that she would be patterned after the one she pursued. She wanted her heart to become one with his.

This is an almost perfect definition of discipleship. We are to be students of Jesus's heart, which we value deeply and which we pursue in order that our hearts might become one with His. But how can we pattern ourselves after His heart unless we are also keenly aware of the state of *our* hearts? We have such powerful blind spots where our own flaws are concerned.

I have a friend who wisely notes, "We tend to judge others by their actions and ourselves by our intentions." In other words, we give ourselves a lot of credit for things we *meant* to do, even if we did not ever get around to doing them. We usually don't offer others the same grace. So how can we mature and improve when we don't evaluate ourselves on accurate scales?

The answer in my life has been *soul friendship*. One of the spiritual disciplines least talked about, soul friendship might be one of the most powerful avenues of growth God has given us.

Before I go into what soul friendship *is*, it is important to discuss what it is *not*. It does not mean being "soul mates," whatever that arbitrary and ubiquitous term has come to mean. Although I started this chapter with an analogy to marriage, I do not want you to get caught in thinking of soul friendship as being unique to marriage. Yes, marriage is soul friendship, but soul friendship is not necessarily marriage. In fact, I would argue that we need at least one soul friend in addition to our spouse. It will both support and enrich our marriages.

And soul friendship is not typical friendship either. Let's explore the differences:

- Typical friendship can be had with anyone of any age. Soul friendship should be had with someone of the same gender. (Soul friends become very close, sharing heart-deep struggles with one another that should stay within the appropriate bounds of friendship, without adding the layer of confusion that would develop by becoming close to someone of the opposite sex.)
- Typical friendship is for the purpose of enjoyment. Soul friendship can be enjoyable, of course, but it exists for the purpose of spiritual development.
- Typical friendship is based on shared interests, even on things as simple as a love of basketball, or cooking, or Rocky movies. Soul friendship may include many shared interests, but it is based on shared purpose—the desire to become like Christ.
- Typical friendship begins with a common experience, whether it be laughter or tears, lunch or travel. Soul friendship begins with a mutual agreement.
- Typical friendship provides opportunities to serve, which you do not *have* to take. You may look like a jerk if you do not mow your friend's yard when he breaks his leg or if you do not bring food when your friend loses a significant loved one, but you do not *have* to do these

things. They are just opportunities to serve. With soul friendship, however, those opportunities to serve become responsibilities to serve, and that is because it all began with a mutual agreement.

What are the responsibilities to serve? As I see it, the responsibilities of a soul friend are to:

1. Pray
2. Listen
3. Encourage
4. Warn
5. Hold the vision

These responsibilities, done well, can take a lot of time and attention. That is why you need only a few soul friends. Jesus had a small group of twelve, but when it came to soul friends, He had three: Peter, James, and John. Three is a good standard. Three is about all anyone can properly care for at one time. Also, it should be noted that not all soul friendships have the same qualities. In my life, I have experienced three kinds of soul friendships, and I can see the biblical correlation for each type.

The first is *constant* soul friendship. A constant soul friendship is intentional but has no end. It is established for an indefinite time or for the general purpose of pursuing spiritual growth. Let me introduce you to my constant soul friend. Journey with me on the "Highway to the Danger Zone," if you will, where my constant soul friendship began: in the early nineties.

With bangs teased to heaven and strategically sprayed, I would leave the house while it was still dark. Becky would be waiting for me at Grandy's, where we met every Wednesday at six in the morning to discuss spiritual matters over biscuits and gravy for an hour. Then we'd head to our high school campus, arriving just before the tardy bell rang.

That was my first taste of soul friendship. Becky and I have only stopped meeting a few brief periods over the almost thirty years that we have been constant soul friends. We have been friends since elementary school and have met to pray weekly since high school. However, it has not always been smooth.

I mentioned the responsibilities of a soul friend. You might have thought that they were easy to accomplish, but responsibilities like "listening" can be more difficult when you consider all of the times that we must listen. For instance, in addition to listening to your soul friend's heartaches and concerns, you must listen to your soul friend's correction and warning. Both of those can be very hard to hear. I have had to listen to Becky's correction more than once, and she has had to listen to mine.

One of her gentle corrections was concerning our decision to meet one morning a week to pray. I was pretty flaky when we were younger, and there were plenty of mornings when I would let Becky sit at Grandy's, eating her breakfast by herself while I stayed tucked in bed. There were no cell phones at the time, so I didn't tell her I wasn't coming. Even when we were in college, and she suggested that we mentor a group of new freshmen girls in prayer, more often than not, I would skip the meetings and never let them know where I was. I'm so embarrassed to think of it now. Becky would ask me with such kindness to show more consideration of her and the girls we were mentoring. She set boundaries too. There were a couple of times when she declined activities with me because she needed to know she could trust the outcome. But she continued to pray for me, continued to be a close friend, and continued to call out my gifts through her affirmation and encouragement on a regular basis. That is what a constant soul friend does.

Years later, she asked for a morning commitment again, when we were in our thirties. She wanted someone to hold her accountable, someone who would pray for her and push her toward a high standard of living for the Kingdom. I agreed, and this time something finally clicked. I have not missed a single meeting except for once or twice when I was sick or out of town.

There was even one morning when Becky was waiting at Starbucks, and after about fifteen minutes of being there alone, she took a photo of the empty chair beside her and texted it to me.

"Hmmm. I wonder who is supposed to be sitting in that chair right now?" she wrote good-naturedly. I jumped up out of bed, threw on my clothes, got to the coffee shop, and we proceeded to have our usual conversation. It was only at the end that I said, "You know we are supposed to meet *tomorrow*, not today, right?"

"What?!" she answered. "Why did you come?"

"Because I owe you!" I said, laughing. It had taken me years to learn the lesson of respecting her time, but once I had learned it, I had learned it for good.

A lot of people use Proverbs 27:17 as a foundational verse for friendship, but I wonder if they understand what it truly means. "As iron sharpens iron," Solomon writes, "so one person sharpens another."

Perhaps we think that we should look for "sharp" friends so that they can perfect us. We want those wise, mature, gracious friends who can contribute to our personalities by inspiring us to be wise, mature, and gracious too. But I tend to look at that verse in a different way now. While I think it is important that we seek out friends with stellar qualities who will be good for us, I also see that a person's shortcomings can be good for us as well. When I have a friend who does everything right, I do not need love, joy, peace, patience, kindness, goodness, or gentleness, and I certainly don't need self-control. I enjoy the friendship so much when it is in a good stage that I cruise along without a care. But when a friend starts exhibiting some flaws, that is when I am on my knees, begging God to grow in me all of the fruit of the Spirit that I can stand. I need patience! I need kindness and gentleness! I need self-control! Double all of those if the person in question is a family member.

A friend's flaws are the hard strike and drag of iron sharpening iron. A friend's flaws sharpen me. But a friend's excellence doesn't hit me hard enough to sharpen much of anything. Someone's imperfections are beneficial in this way. It's ironic that the one thing that makes me want to run away is usually what God has given me as a gift in disguise.

Sure, Becky's patience made me a better friend in the long run, but when she asked God to help her be patient with me in the meantime, she was made better as well. That is iron sharpening iron.

But watch out for these kind of thoughts:

That person is wearing me out.

They never do what they say they're going to do. I'm done.

I don't have to be treated this way.

These statements may be lies from the enemy that will remove from you the opportunity to become better and sharper and more filled with the fruit of the Spirit. They remove from you the opportunity to see real and lasting change in your loved one too.

These days Becky and I meet over coffee in the morning or afternoon or whenever she is not running her kids to and from school or practice. Sometimes we can linger for an hour and a half, and sometimes we grab a ten-minute phone conversation. We can do the latter only because we have learned how to focus quickly. We get right to the point without a lot of small talk. Of course, some phone conversations and times together are just for fun, but that once-a-week meeting, however enjoyable it may be, has a target. That purpose is to keep one another on track in our pursuit of the Kingdom of God.

During a particularly busy time when her kids were sick, I told Becky we could postpone our meeting for a couple of weeks. She quickly responded, "Nika, no. If I start postponing our meeting until I find a better, more convenient time, I won't see you again for another eighteen years, when my last child graduates high school. And maybe not even then."

There will never be an opportune time to cultivate soul friends.

A biblical example of a constant soul friendship would be the connection between David and Jonathan. Like any strong soul friendship, theirs began with a mutual agreement. It was not a casual relationship of two people who have many things in common. There was more between them: supreme respect. It was a respect that created a bond that would remain even long after Jonathan's death, when David cared for Jonathan's son.[7]

Even the details of the mutual agreement are given to us, though not the exact words, although I think they are obvious. We read about it in 1 Samuel 18:3–4:

> And Jonathan made a solemn pact with David, because he loved him as he loved himself. Jonathan sealed the pact by taking off his robe and giving it to David, together with his tunic, sword, bow, and belt. (NLT)

There was great meaning in the transference of these gifts. It was a display of one of the most important aspects of a soul friendship: holding the vision. You see, David had been anointed by the prophet Samuel to become the next king of Israel. There was only one problem: David was *not* the natural successor. Israel already had a king named Saul, and his son—the rightful heir to the throne—was none other than Jonathan. The mutual agreement that was explicitly communicated between these two soul friends when Jonathan gave David all of his belongings, including his weapons, was this: "I acknowledge your divine anointing, David. I agree to see you as God sees you, not as men see you. I will hold the vision that God has given you for your future. I hereby forfeit my natural right to be the next king of Israel in deference to your supernatural right to be the next king of Israel. Here is my cloak; you may take my place. Here are my weapons; I will not oppose you."

David came into Jonathan's presence dressed as a shepherd. When he left, he was robed like a prince. He came as vulnerable as a commoner. When he left, he was equipped like a king. This is the finest example of soul friendship. Both friends must make a commitment to view one another through God's eyes and hold the vision He has given them for the future.

The second type of soul friendship is *seasonal* soul friendship. It can be intense for a while. A seasonal soul friendship is established for a specific time and for the particular purpose of pursuing a spiritual aim. The decision to be soul friends accelerates the usual progression of friendship.

I have enjoyed a seasonal soul friendship with Candy, whom you read about in the previous chapter. I also have experienced a sweet seasonal soul friendship with Allison. I came alongside both of them in pursuit of a promise God had spoken to them.

Allison and her husband, Ricky, had three biological children when they found out about a family having some difficulties caring for their three children. They were eager to give those kids a temporary home. Around the same time, Allison gave birth to their fourth child, making seven kids under the same roof.

They spent the next four years praying and working toward reuniting the three children with their biological family, but eventually it became apparent that this would not be possible. Ricky and Allison sensed a shifting in their hearts, and they realized that the Lord was guiding them to adopt the three dear children they had come to love as their own. There were many challenges and significant periods of waiting as they followed God's voice. There were days when Allison felt weary and heartsore from the process, and she wondered if she had been mistaken in what she'd heard from the Lord. She waited for reassurance.

We were at a conference at church when she came over and knelt by my chair. "During the worship tonight, I thought of you. I think the Lord wants you to tell me something. Can you think of what that would be?"

I had no reference point at all. Allison and I hardly knew one another. I said, "Well, I don't think so, Allison. I will pray for you and your situation, though. I'll let you know if anything comes to mind."

Two years passed.

Allison continued to seek God's detailed direction for her family. Meanwhile, I, too, was feeling frustrated with several things in my life. One day when I was praying, I felt the Lord saying that I was being disobedient in the task He had given me as a writer. He had put the content for a book about hope on my heart. But there were a lot of days when I was not writing at all. I wasn't "showing up for work." I asked Him what to do about that, and He brought Allison to my mind. We would have considered ourselves friends, but we had not talked about anything beyond the normal superficial catch-up in the church lobby. However, as soon as I thought of her, I knew I needed to have an appointment once or twice a month with her to be honest about the stewardship of my time. I needed to give an account of it.

By the way, Allison is an accountant.

As I was dialing her number, I realized that *there was* something God wanted me to tell her two years earlier. But it wasn't about her heavenly assignment. It was about mine.

When I contacted her, she could not have been more excited to begin praying for me and asking meaningful questions about my writing process on a regular basis. But she also was hoping that I could pray for her. We began praying intensely for the changes in their family. They continued to seek hope, even as they felt turned in a new direction.

"I'm in conditions of low visibility," she said. "I'm looking ahead, and I can't see what's next. We think we know where God is guiding us as a family, but I just can't see how it will all come together."

Allison and I joined as sisters in prayer. We began meeting twice a month in the foyer of our church to pray about her family and to pray about my next book. We were both intentionally going after what the Lord had spoken to us. We were both pursuing a promise. The year we focused in prayer we saw the completion and launch of my book, *Hunting Hope*, plus the completion of two other manuscripts, including the book you are reading right now. We saw Allison's friends band together to buy her family a twelve-passenger van, and for the first time in two years, Allison and Ricky were able to ride to church or take a road trip with their family in *one* car instead of two. Obstacle after obstacle disintegrated before them.

Now they are no longer pursuing the promise. They are living in it. Today, the adoption is complete, and they are the family of nine that the Lord had told them they would be. Both Allison and I would say that our seasonal soul friendship played a critical role in receiving our promises.

A biblical example of seasonal soul friendship is Joshua and Caleb. These two men went on a mission to conquer Canaan as partners and leaders. The mission was for a specific time and a particular purpose: to pursue a promise. During the mission, they prayed powerfully and relied on one another for support and encouragement. Because of their soul friendship, they were able to do things that would not have been possible otherwise. They remained close friends, but eventually that mission came to an end, and so did the level of intensity of their seasonal soul friendship.

The third type of soul friendship is an *interrupted* soul friendship. This type of soul friendship is one that was established on godly principles and intentions, but has been interrupted because of sin or discord.

I am currently in two interrupted soul friendships. These unrelated friends are engaged in sin that is cutting them off from new life. They do not live a revelatory, free, purposed, productive, guided, and community-filled life in the Spirit. They are not cut off from the love of God, though. Nothing can separate them from that.[8] What is *my* response during this time? I see myself as a lighthouse while they are out on a dark and tumultuous sea, and I continually circle around and back again to shine a light on the image of Christ in them. They are created to look like Him; we all are. With one friend, I have continued casual communication, though

I do not make mention of critical spiritual matters. With the other friend, there is no communication, though not by my choice. In either case, my position remains the same: I stand stationary and dependable like a lighthouse, holding to the vision of who God says they are and what He desires for their future. I pray for them, viewing them with eyes like the Lord, eyes that see these friends as the Lord sees them, not as they are now.

A biblical example of an interrupted soul friendship is Jesus and Peter. Jesus saw Peter as immovable and reliable as a mighty rock, and He told him so.[9] So when Peter made some choices that were exactly the opposite of who the Lord designed him to be, both shame and circumstances interrupted their soul friendship for a time. But Christ continued to hold the rock-solid vision of Peter at his best, and that is who Peter eventually became.

Following Jesus's example, if we continue to hold the vision of Christ's plan in an interrupted soul friendship, there is a good chance of reconciliation. The eyes through which we "view" that person may help determine who they become. May our highest prayer be to see them as God sees them, for His life is the life they were destined to live at the Creation of the world.

The enemy would like us to abandon the people in our lives when times get tough. He knows that community is God's supreme design. Our God is three-in-one. His existence is the very definition of soul friendship. No wonder the enemy sets himself against unity with a fiery passion.

Stand by your soul friends. If you do not have one, pray that God will lead you into a meaningful soul friendship, and then start *being* a soul friend. Don't wait for someone to come to you. You may have to take a vulnerable step and ask someone to join you in the intentional pursuit of the Kingdom. Your newborn friendship may feel awkward at first, but there is a principle to new life: all things grow. Whether positive or negative, the relationships in our lives will reach a state of maturity.

You never bring just one person into your life. They come with the words and wisdom of all the people they know. Sometimes they come with the *actual* people! You will find your friends multiplying with or without your permission. Good friends will bring more good friends into your life. Bad friends will bring more bad friends.

Sure, we should befriend people of all kinds.

But since we know that friends reproduce according to their kind, we must make sure our *closest* friends are good seeds.

The Sixth Day, Morning

Then God said, "Let the earth produce every sort of animal,
each producing offspring of the same kind—
livestock, small animals that scurry along the ground,
and wild animals." And that is what happened.
God made all sorts of wild animals, livestock,
and small animals, each able to produce offspring
of the same kind. And God saw that it was good.

—

GENESIS 1:24–25 NLT

Jesus designs jaws, and claws, and manes. He gives giraffes prehensile tongues and monkeys prehensile tails. He forms horns and tusks and hooves. He crowns the ram and makes his feet steady for the mountains. He places a headdress on the lion and makes his feet swift for the savannah.

He smooths a panther's satin coat; puts terror in the teeth of a tiger; latches percussion to a rattlesnake; hangs a trumpet on an elephant; sets the alarm clock inside a bear.

The Creator who gives speed to a gazelle offers patience to a sloth; hands humor to a baboon and mischief to a chimpanzee; fastens a pristine collar to a mallard's neck; designs the chameleon's skin to change and the frog's skin to molt; plans the stubby pace of a hedgehog and the gangly gait of a giraffe.

He crafts a kitten's tiny cry, and a puppy's playful tail. He teaches a joey to stay in his mother's pouch, and a duckling to stay in his mother's steps.

"Let the earth produce animals, each reproducing itself," He says.

On Day Six, God festoons the land with a zoo.

THIRTEEN

Let There Be More Life

WHEN GOD SAW all that He had made, He said it was good. *Good* is God's favorite adjective.

Even so, animals never will be anything close to a human. This is because they are not triune, like God. It is clear that they are intelligent and have emotions. Obviously, they have souls that think and feel, as well as bodies. However, they cannot carry God's image because they do not have spirits. Therefore, they have not been given the authority we have been given. King David wrote about this in awe:

When I look at the night sky and see the work of your
  fingers—
    the moon and the stars you set in place—
what are mere mortals that you should think about them,
    human beings that you should care for them?
Yet you made them only a little lower than God
    and crowned them with glory and honor.

You gave them charge of everything you made,
    putting all things under their authority—
the flocks and the herds
    and all the wild animals,
the birds in the sky, the fish in the sea,
    and everything that swims the ocean currents.
O LORD, our Lord, your majestic name fills the earth![1]

God entrusted His masterpiece to mankind, giving us unquestionable dominion over the animals. The next key factor in new life is authority.

God's glory is shown to the world through authority, both ours and His. The world can see His when we display ours. These days, authority is a tricky concept to discuss, but we are the only ones walking on eggshells about the topic. We are the only ones ignoring it. Satan isn't. I think there is a reason that authority has become so difficult for us to talk about and live from, and that is because Satan has a strategy to strip from God His glory. This could never happen in truth or reality. But it certainly happens in what we perceive. The less we live in proper alignment with authority, the less we see of God's glory.

A perfect example of sidestepping authority is in the story of conquering Canaan I mentioned in the previous chapter. When the Israelites were commanded to take the promised land, they hesitated, even though God had told them they would be successful if they did what He was asking them to do. They muttered, "Yes, but how?" They asked too many questions. They postponed too long.

Finally, God said, "Enough!" And He disciplined them. What did they do when He disciplined them?

They suddenly hustled to obey like toddlers who've been threatened with time-out. They said, "Wait! Wait! We'll go!" and they started off to Canaan to obey the Lord's order, but Moses said, "Where are you going? That won't work now."

They all headed out anyway. Moses just stayed where he was and watched them. Sure enough, they suffered many losses and retreated in defeat. The same things can happen to us if we shirk God's authority and wait to obey. Please realize that some commands have an expiration date. Whatever He asks you to do, do it as soon as possible. Particular opportunities are only for right now. Take hold of them or they will melt like manna at midday. Because God is eternal, we often think that He will wait on us forever, but He won't.

When we hear God's authoritative voice, it is always for our good. Sometimes God tells us to tear down and sometimes He asks us to build up. When we tear down, we can see the thing that needs tearing down, but when we build up, we do not always see the thing we must build. It is just a hope or a promise that God has given us for our future. It is planting, and that requires holding on to a vision when there is nothing but a bleak landscape in our view. Building up necessitates believing that one day Eden will thrive where right now there is only dust. There are many days between a seed and flower, and during those days, we wait.

While we wait, we must use our mouths as conduits for God's will in our lives. Speaking His Word over ourselves and our situations is one of the most significant ways that we exercise the authority we have been given. If we, the sons and daughters of God, do not speak His Word out loud, who is going to? We have everything we need to live a new life, but we must realize our authority as His chosen children in order for this to happen.

Do you have any idea how powerful we are? The Bible tells us that John the Baptist was the greatest prophet who ever lived, yet even the least of us now in the Kingdom is greater than he is![2] What does that mean? There is only one reason we could be greater than John the Baptist, and it is our authority. John the Baptist spoke the words of Jesus through the power of the Holy Spirit, although he died before knowing the risen Christ. But we do know Him! Now that Jesus has defeated death for all time and chosen to live inside us, what is under His feet is under *our* feet.

How sad it is when we look back with envy on biblical accounts of men and women who seemed to have a direct connection to know God's will for them. Today, we not only have the Spirit, we have the resurrection power of Jesus living in us. The people of old needed to know God's will for them, but today God "works in [us] to will and to act in order to fulfill his good purpose."[3] We don't have to worry about figuring out God's will when we abide in Him. He will work in us to accomplish what He desires. We have access to God's power in a way that no other generation before us has. Job moaned, "How small a whisper do we hear of him! But the thunder of his power who can understand?"[4]

You and I have more than Job had. Today we not only hear His whisper; we can know the thunder of His power. Today God is able, "through his mighty power at work within us, to accomplish infinitely more than we might ask or think."[5]

Please stop wishing God would speak to you the way He spoke to Abraham and Noah. Only the enemy would have us pine for an older time that we have far surpassed. The Bible tells us that previous generations of faith died without receiving the promise. They only saw it from a distance.[6] We have it easier, not harder.

But we have to rely on His authority in order to exercise ours. That means we must agree with His Word and obey it.

My career didn't flourish until I got into alignment with God's authority and started using my own. My whole life I have prayed that one day I would be able to write books that powerfully encourage Christians in their callings, but my career kept starting and stopping. I know that teaching through writing is one of my assignments from God, but it was many years before I actually wrote a book. It was as if there were a giant invisible obstacle in front of me. I didn't feel worthy of writing a book. I didn't think anyone would like it or want to read it. In my case, there was a lot of tearing down that needed to happen, as well as a lot of building up. I had to tear down my fear and build up my sense of worth as a child of God.

I sensed the Lord telling me to pray out loud, but I didn't want to. In fact, I felt I couldn't. I would try to speak aloud, but then I would stammer or whisper or wimp out. If I had been afraid of voicing daring prayers out loud to people, that would have been understandable. The bizarre thing is that I was not willing to speak those prayers out loud when I was alone either. I was terrified to bring the desires of my heart out into the atmosphere. What if they were never realized?

I guess I thought if my hopes were never spoken, my heart couldn't be broken.

There is a reason for the mark of fear on speaking our desires and Kingdom assignments out loud. The enemy knows that the Creator did not *think* the world into being. He *spoke* it into being. God has invited us to co-create with Him by speaking His Word. Satan knows that if he can just keep us doing our best prayer in our thought life, we might not be working with God as much we think we are. Satan came "to steal and kill and destroy"[7] our co-creation with God, which is our destiny as His sons and daughters.

Though I tried to resist, I knew God was wanting me to speak prayers out loud, so I went outdoors. Outdoors, words can be sucked away, like the shuttle in a bank teller's tube. By praying outdoors, I was counting on my prayers being zipped upward to God. No one else would hear them. I couldn't even bear to hear my own heart-deep words, so I wore headphones and played praise music while I prayed. Needing some structure for my prayers, I created a little playlist, with each song representing a different request. So I walked, praying through the playlist of prayer themes. It is interesting that when I started saying those out-loud prayers in earnest, I chose to walk around the church building of my youth, the place I had attended for twenty-nine years of my life. For four months, I prayed around and around that building, every other day. I enjoy variety, so a few times I tried to go to a neighborhood park to pray, but it didn't feel right. It was as if a magnet were pulling me back to the same spot, even though I no longer attended church there.

Because the draw was so strong, I decided to ask God if there was any significance to it. I said, "Lord, why do I keep coming back here?" I sensed an answer immediately.

I'm taking you back to where the seeds were planted.

As soon as I heard that, I saw a picture in my mind. It was a memory from about age twelve. An army of men and women with shovels were walking across a dusty field in their church clothes. It was the day we all walked from our previous church building to the plot of land that would become the building I was walking around. Back then, there was nothing but a bleak landscape and a group of people with a vision. We prayed for God to do amazing things with a grand building through which He would call people to Himself. Then we positioned our blades and began to dig.

And in the middle of the crowd, there was a little girl who already knew she wanted to be a writer. Into the soil we opened as the family of God, I threw in one, tiny seed:

"God, if You can, use me too."

Tears filled my eyes when I realized that it had been thirty years since I had prayed that prayer. And God still remembered it.

Of course He did.

The prayers that I frightfully prayed out loud at age forty-two were the same that I boldly prayed out loud at age twelve, back when I was too young to know the despair of unfulfilled dreams. God not only remembers those bookend prayers, He remembers all of the prayers I journaled and thought and cried out in the years in between. How many prayers did it take? I don't know, but I do know this:

Only one prayer was enough, but all of them were necessary.

It was through the long process of praying to become a writer that I finally believed I was one. The prayers weren't about changing God's mind; they were about changing mine.

The wait has been long, but God's timing is perfect. These two realities can co-exist in your life.

Please know that the prayers you are praying out loud are creating something that wasn't there before. You exercise your authority as a son or daughter of the King by listening to His Spirit and repeating His Word to yourself out loud.

Repeat it.

Obey it.

Wait on it.

That is the simple plan for new life.

No other passage in the Bible explains new life better than the eighth chapter of Romans. In the chapter just before it, we read the famously wishy-washy words of Paul when he grieves that he doesn't do what he wants to and does do what he doesn't want to. Chapter 7 is a passage that whimpers with defeat. But it is followed by the glorious chapter 8, a section that rings with victory. Because we have discussed the difference between body, soul, and spirit, in the verses below I have taken the liberty of altering one word in this passage to increase our understanding. We know that our *spirits* are our true identity in Christ, and our *souls* are our mind, will, and emotion. Our souls are what we think, desire, and feel. We can also refer to this as *the flesh*.

We assume that we are driven by our souls, but the Bible tells us clearly that we are not. Our minds, wills, and emotions will try to boss us around. But our spirits do not have to obey our souls.

The basic evidence of this is when we are tempted to steal something. Our will chooses the object of our desire. Our emotions bring pleasure at the desire. Our minds devise a plan to achieve that desire. This is how it happens with lying, adultery, and every sin. But, as I have said previously, a sinful desire may enter, but we do not have to entertain it. This is exactly what Paul describes in Romans 8. Think carefully about this passage as you read it.

> Those who are dominated by the [soul] think about sinful things, but those who are controlled by the Holy Spirit think about things that please the Spirit. So letting your [soul] control your mind leads to death. But letting the

Spirit control your mind leads to life and peace. *For the [soul] is always hostile to God. It never did obey God's laws, and it never will.* That's why those who are still under the control of their [soul] can never please God.

But you are not controlled by your [soul]. You are controlled by the Spirit if you have the Spirit of God living in you. (And remember that those who do not have the Spirit of Christ living in them do not belong to him at all.) And Christ lives within you, so even though your body will die because of sin, the Spirit gives you life because you have been made right with God. The Spirit of God, who raised Jesus from the dead, lives in you. And just as God raised Christ Jesus from the dead, he will give life to your mortal bodies by this same Spirit living within you.

Therefore, dear brothers and sisters, *you have no obligation to do what your [soul] urges you to do.* For if you live by its dictates, you will die. But if through the power of the Spirit you put to death the deeds of your [soul], you will live. For all who are led by the Spirit of God are children of God.[8]

Did you absorb that? We are now free from a terrible pattern. We can stop trying to punish our souls into doing the right thing. We have been trying to make a human soul do something it cannot do. Our souls never have obeyed God's laws, and they never will.

By the authority of the Spirit, we have authority over our souls.

Now that we are walking in revelation, freedom, purpose, productivity, guidance, and community, it is vital that we realize the authority we have been given. As you write and repeat this declaration, you are announcing that God's plans for you will stand.

But in order for that to happen, we must submit to His authority. Stop resisting and let Him work through you. As you embrace God's authority, He will give you some of your own.

Let There Be Authority
(from Jeremiah 1:4-10 NLT)

The Lord gave me this message:

"I knew you before I formed you in your mother's womb, _____. Before you were born I set you apart and appointed you as my prophet to the nations."

"O Sovereign Lord," I said, "I can't speak for you! I'm too _____ (insert your fear or flaw)!"

The Lord replied, "Don't say, 'I'm too _____ (insert your fear or flaw),' for you must go wherever I send you and say whatever I tell you. And don't be afraid of the people, for I will be with you and will protect you. I, the Lord, have spoken!"

Then the Lord reached out and touched my mouth and said, "Look, I have put my words in your mouth! Today I appoint you to stand up against nations and kingdoms. Some you must uproot and tear down, destroy and overthrow. Others you must build up and plant."

One of my favorite stories about the mysterious act of giving voice to our prayers almost didn't happen because I was afraid to pray out loud. Several years ago, I had resigned from my nine-to-five job in order to pursue writing full time. I am also a speaker and an education consultant, but all of those streams of income are irregular. There were months when my budget was tight. There were even more months when there was no budget because there was no money to budget. During one of those periods, I was invited to work with an organization to tutor struggling high school student writers for twelve days. When I accepted the temporary position from the administrator, he informed me that I would later need to negotiate the terms of compensation with the authority of the project, someone higher than he.

I do not like to negotiate. I was hoping they would just tell me how much they were willing to pay for the twelve days of tutoring and let me get on with it. But we scheduled the negotiation meeting over lunch.

On my way to the restaurant, I was distraught. I wasn't sure I could eat because I was so upset by the idea of negotiating. I kept praying as I drove, "Please don't make me negotiate, Lord! Please! I don't want to haggle back and forth. I know I am good at what I do, but I hardly have the courage to ask for what I think it is worth. Please let this man decide on a fair figure without me having to say a word!"

I have worked in education consultation with universities, public and private schools, and educational organizations for ten years, so I am very familiar with the typical compensation. In fact, I had worked with this organization before, and my first guess was that for twelve days of work, the maximum they would offer was $1,500. It was a fair wage for the type of work I would be doing.

But I wasn't sure they would give me that much unless I asked for it. So I prayed silently, "Lord, will You please give me $1,500? I know that is the maximum of what they will offer. You know I don't like negotiating. I'm asking You to move them to offer me $1,500, without my having to ask for it."

One of my favorite verses in the Bible is Proverbs 21:1: "In the LORD's hand the king's heart is a stream of water that he channels toward all who please him." I depend on God to move those in authority to show me kindness and special approval. I am not shy about asking God to channel their blessings toward me. On the day of the negotiation, I was driving to meet a "king" in his field. Many people had remarked that he was intimidating to them. I had never met him, but I needed God not only to *free me* from fear of him but also to *free him* to show me favor. I wanted God to turn his heart like a stream of water.

As I was praying, God asked me, *How much do you want?*

I answered in my thoughts, "I need a $1,500 offer . . . except that is not really enough to make ends meet this month . . . so maybe a little more?"

He answered so clearly, *Double it.*

I prayed in my head, "Okay, I would like $3,000, Lord. But that will never happen unless You provide some kind of miracle. I know this organization, and they would never give me that much for twelve days of work, even though I know that what I can accomplish with these students is worth it. But I'll go ahead and ask You for $3,000. Anything is possible with You."

He spoke again, *Say it out loud.*

I froze. My chest became tight. I did not have the courage to say that figure out loud, even in the isolation of my own car. But I had heard the Lord so clearly.

I whimpered, "I would like $3,000, Lord. Um . . . please."

He answered instantly, *Double it.*

"What?! That is just ridiculous!" I went back to praying in my head. "There is no way they are going to offer me $3,000, much less $6,000! I mean, I am not even sure they are going to want to offer me $1,500 in the first place! Come on! This seems like a cruel game to ask me to consider numbers like these. But, okay. I need $6,000, Lord. And I ask it in Your name. I choose to be in alignment with what You are doing."

Tears started running down my cheeks.

Say it out loud, He said.

I couldn't. I just couldn't. There was not a soul who would ever know of our conversation, but I could not make myself utter such a hope-filled request out loud to God.

Pulling into the parking lot of the restaurant, I slowed down. Was I really about to ignore God's request? I know His voice, and I knew He was asking me to do it. Was I really about to walk away without risking the trust it takes for a miracle?

No, I wasn't.

I said out loud, "Lord, I need $6,000." I don't know how to explain it, but I sensed He was smiling at the sound of my faith rising. Then, hitting my steering wheel with my fist, I shouted, "I want $6,000!"

Boy, I felt stupid. I parked the car and went inside.

The lunch went well. The man who had seemed so intimidating in the first few moments of our meeting showed great interest in my experience and skills. I was at ease when I realized we were like-minded in our approach of teaching hard-to-reach student populations. As the waitress took our plates away at the end, he said, "Nika, I knew you were probably a good fit for us based on your qualifications, but now I am *sure* you are the perfect fit based on your heart for students. We would be happy to offer you $1,500 for your work with us. Does that sound reasonable to you?"

I paused. It was reasonable. From the very beginning, I had thought that figure was what they would offer me. But after being bolstered in faith during the car ride to the restaurant, I didn't think that was what God was wanting me to accept. It was time for my one big stab at negotiation: "Well . . . ," I said slowly.

I tried to think of something else to say.

"Oh, I have insulted you," he interrupted quickly. "Let me adjust my offer. We are prepared to pay you $12,000. Does that sound reasonable to you?"

Trying to hide my widened eyes, I answered, "Yes. Thank you, sir." I swallowed hard and shook his hand. He had settled on ten times more than his original offer, and I had only said one word.

I hardly turned out of the parking lot before I was hollering, and laughing, and praising. God had asked me to double the first figure and say it out loud, then He had asked me to double the second figure and say it out loud, then He had doubled the third figure Himself.

And I heard it as clearly as if He had said it out loud.

If you believe that your Helper, the Holy Spirit, is on your side; if you believe that your Champion, Jesus, is still alive and is living in you; if you believe that your Father, Jehovah, loves you with an everlasting love, then say it out loud in declarative prayer as often as possible. Prayer and fasting are the golden setting into which Jesus drops this diamond: "Store your treasures in heaven, where moths and rust cannot destroy, and thieves do not break in and steal. Wherever your treasure is, there the desires of your heart will also be."[9]

By telling us to store our treasures in heaven, He is telling us to put all our hope in God. He is telling us to pray.

We will never find answers for our brokenness through earthly means. They are only accessible through the Spirit of God. By speaking His words, we are admitting that we already have all that we need in Him, and we are made whole. By the authority of Christ, we walk in authority. By His power, we walk in power.

This certainly goes for our words. The Bible warns us that "if anyone speaks, they should do so as one who speaks the very words of God."[10] What power we have been given! God says His Word will achieve the purpose for which it was sent.[11] Not a single word we say and pray in His name will be wasted. One day God will declare, *Child, while you were hoping, I was helping. While you were praying, I was preparing. And while you were waiting, I was working.*

At the right time, He will open the doors of our situations and show us the treasure that our prayers have been building for us.

FOURTEEN

Authority

AUTHORITY IS EXTREMELY DANGEROUS if you don't know how to wear it.

To illustrate, I will paint a picture of myself as the self-made Cinderella of eighth grade.

White jeans are where it's at. All the girls in my class have them. I don't have a pair of white jeans, even though I have begged and begged my mother. She will not buy a pair, no matter how many times I ask. Now, being the resourceful girl I am, I reason that I may not have white jeans, but I *do* have blue jeans and bleach. So on a Wednesday afternoon, as I'm walking home from school, I think, *I'll just throw some blue jeans into the bathtub with a gallon of Clorox, and then wear me some new white jeans to church tonight. Yeah!*

It's a plan. I leave the jeans soaking for half an hour and then wring them out, run them in the dryer, and I'm good to go. Rinsing the jeans never crosses my mind, but it will cross my derriere before the night is through. I throw on the jeans, grinning as I apply my Kissing Potion rollerball lip gloss. I tease those bangs up. I look fourteen-fabulous.

I go to church in my oh-so-clean-white jeans. After I am there about twenty minutes, I notice the jeans are not looking so clean and white anymore. They are kind of looking like Hellmann's mayonnaise. They are smelling like Hellmann's mayonnaise too, but I ignore it. I chalk up the slightly off color to the fluorescent lights, and don't think of my jeans again until the tops of my thighs erupt in flames. When I look down to see what has caused the sudden burning and itching, I find the color has changed again. If they made a Crayola crayon from the color these jeans have become, they could safely call it electric urine. In fact, the smell the jeans are emitting could be called electric urine as well. I think, *This is going wrong. Very wrong. It has to be as bad as it gets.*

But, no, this story will not reach its miserable climax until ten minutes later, when my jeans begin disappearing before my eyes. They disintegrate, melting into thin air . . . or melting into my skin, I am not sure which. The holes start small and grow by the minute. If anything touches these now bus-yellow jeans—which have begun to smell like a toxic waste dump—they rip apart. This is unfortunate, because at this point I am clawing at my legs in desperation. The sting is relentless. My knees have become raw flesh. My rear end is on FI-YER. As the Bible teacher continues teaching, the holes in my jeans grow and grow, and all I can think about is getting to the car before the clock runs out . . .

(And that is the end of this "scary tale" for you, my friend. Sorry.)

The moral is this: Some things shouldn't be faked.

Oh, and also: The average person has no real concept of the chemical potency of household bleach.

I share this memory because it is a perfect example of what can happen when someone who is inexperienced tries to wear something dangerously powerful. It is best to understand what you are putting on yourself.

Consider the armor of God.

Many people who try to "put on" the most authoritative garment of all time have no idea what they are doing. I used to be one of them. In the past, if I were going to do something important, such as get on a stage to speak or get on a plane to travel, I would think, *Wait! I have got to put on the armor of God before I begin!*

Then I would quote from memory Ephesians 6:13–17:

Therefore put on the full armor of God, so that when the day of evil comes, you may be able to stand your ground, and after you have done everything, to stand. Stand firm then, with the belt of truth buckled around your waist, with the breastplate of righteousness in place, and with your feet fitted with the readiness that comes from the gospel of peace. In addition to all this, take up the shield of faith, with which you can extinguish all the flaming arrows of the evil one. Take the helmet of salvation and the sword of the Spirit, which is the word of God.

I would confidently do this again and again. Then something happened that would forever shift my understanding of what it means to put on the full armor of God. I was with an acquaintance of mine who is a Christian but who was living in blatant sin, in total disregard of what God clearly outlines in the Bible. She was about to embark on something significant, so she stopped and quoted aloud this passage about the armor of God. I was stunned. I could not help but think, *She is not obeying several of the commands God has given in His Word. She wants to pick and choose which parts of the Bible to adhere to. How can she employ this section of Scripture for her benefit when she has not adhered to any other passage? It doesn't work that way.*

When we take a step off of the path of obedience that God has for us, wandering into enemy territory, why would we think that just saying words from Ephesians 6 would protect us? That couldn't be what the armor means. God says we are protected when we stay on His path for us and follow what He says. He never meant for us to *say* a string of sentences and think that we would be fine, no matter what we *do*.

Think about the link between authority and a uniform.

The presence of a police officer changes the atmosphere. When law enforcement walks into the room, everyone notices. If a police vehicle pulls up onto the road, everyone slows down. Before the officer has said a word, the uniform has spoken. Before the red and blue lights flash, the black-and-white paint has given the signal.

> The uniform worn by a police officer elicits stereotypes about that person's status, authority, attitudes, and motivations. The police uniform identifies a person with powers to arrest and use force. . . . The police uniform can have extraordinary psychological and physical impact. Depending on the background of the citizen, the police uniform can elicit emotions ranging from pride and respect, to fear and anger.[12]

This is not necessarily about the threat of weapons either. Think about the last time you saw police officers directing traffic on foot. There they were, wearing the signature peaked caps and neon-orange vests. You could not even see the rest of the uniform. You were driving a car that weighs two tons, but you obeyed the hand gestures of a man with a whistle.

He could not have chased you.

When you stopped or turned at his command, you were not submitting to the man himself, because you did not know him and you were not afraid of him. If the same man had been making the same gestures, but was wearing a pair of dirty jeans and a Krispy Kreme T-shirt, you would have ignored him or honked, but you certainly would not have submitted to him. Yet you submitted to a man wearing a police uniform because of the authority he represents.

In the same way, the presence of a Christian changes the atmosphere. We have the power to arrest and use force in the spiritual realm. When we walk into a room, the enemy notices. Before we have said a word, the armor of God has spoken. Believe me, Satan is not submitting to *us*. We are just a guy in a donut shirt. Satan submits to Christians who are wearing the armor of God because of the authority we represent.

By the way, one of the most enlightening things I noticed while reading about the psychology of police uniforms is that people in a sudden crisis or need begin scanning a crowd for a police uniform instantly. The moment they find one, they feel safe. People think, *The police officer will help me. He will know what to do!*

I like that. An officer is charged with protecting and serving the community. And so is a believer. I pray that people in a sudden crisis or need begin scanning the crowd for a Christian instantly. And the moment they find one, I hope they feel safe. I want people to think, *The Christian will help me. He will know what to do!*

The armor of God is not just for us. We are not here only to arrest and use force in the heavens; we are here to protect and serve on the earth. Now reflect on the connection between authority and protection.

The police officer is protected by her uniform. Even if someone did not take heed of the badge and the blue, there are weapons: handcuffs, a baton, a Taser, pepper spray, a window punch, and a gun. An officer is authorized to use all of these forms of protection in the line of duty.

That is, of course, until she breaks the very law she represents. Then the officer becomes a civilian and is divested of both the authority and the protection of the uniform.

We must understand that the armor of God carries with it some responsibilities as well. If we want the authority and the protection of the uniform, we must honor the One we represent. Putting on the armor of God is a way of life. It is not a magic spell, or an incantation, or a chant. And we can't use it that way. Wearing the armor of God looks like this:

God tells us to buckle the belt of truth around our waists. Jesus says He is the Truth.[13] *Therefore, the belt of truth is Jesus.* Until we have chosen to put Jesus first in our lives, we are unprotected.

God tells us to put the breastplate of righteousness in place. "The one who does what is right is righteous, just as [Jesus] is righteous."[14] Doing what is right is obedience. *Therefore, the breastplate of righteousness is obeying Jesus.* It is impossible for us to live a flawless life. Yet we continually move in the direction of perfection, and we are protected when we think and act like Jesus.

God tells us to fit our feet with the readiness that comes from the gospel of peace. "[Jesus] himself is our peace. . . . His purpose was to create in himself one new humanity out of the two, thus making peace."[15] *Therefore, the gospel of peace is unity in Jesus.* We cannot live in division and strife and think that we are protected. The enemy enjoys disagreement like it's a playground.

God tells us to take up the helmet of salvation. What is that? We find out in Philippians 4:6: "Do not be anxious about anything, but in every situation, by prayer and petition, with thanksgiving, present your requests to God." When we present our concerns to the Lord, our thinking is transformed. We stop trying to handle it and surrender to the Spirit. That is what it means to have the mind of Christ.[16] *Therefore, the helmet of salvation is prayer in the name of Jesus.* Presenting our requests to God guards our hearts and minds. Leaving it to Him is a protection.

God tells us to take up the shield of faith. "Faith comes from hearing, that is, hearing the Good News about Christ."[17] *Therefore, the shield of faith is believing the words of Jesus.* It is exposing ourselves to sound preaching, teaching, and reading the Bible. If we know what Jesus says and believe it, then when Satan launches all manner of lies in our direction, we will recognize them and extinguish them.

God tells us to take up the sword of the Spirit. "The word of God is alive and powerful. It is sharper than the sharpest two-edged sword. . . . It exposes our innermost thoughts and desires."[18] The Word was not meant to be used against others, but against us. Its purpose is to penetrate us, to divide our souls and spirits, so that nothing in all creation is hidden from God's sight. *Therefore, the sword of the Spirit is agreement with Jesus.* Staying in agreement is the best battle strategy of all.

This is the reality of the armor of God. God did not mean for us to put it on by reciting a memory verse while failing to live it out. That would be as dangerous as wearing straight-bleached jeans; it wouldn't work for long. We are protected by the armor of God when we *choose Jesus* above ourselves, *obey Jesus* through our actions, *pursue unity in Jesus* in all of our relationships, *pray in the name of Jesus* and give our concerns to God, *believe the words of Jesus* as we expose ourselves to sound teaching, and *agree with the words of Jesus* by turning the Word onto ourselves. That is how we defeat the enemy, not *out there*, but on the real battlefield, *in here*. Stop letting Satan tell you who you are.

Let God tell your spirit who you are. Then let your spirit tell your soul who you are. Then let your soul tell your body who you are. Finally, let your body language and words tell the world who you are.

God gave us authority over our bodies:
- "And so, dear brothers and sisters, I plead with you to give your bodies to God because of all he has done for you."[19]
- "So whether you eat or drink, or whatever you do, do it all for the glory of God."[20]

God gave us authority over our minds:
- "And now, dear brothers and sisters, one final thing. Fix your thoughts on what is true, and honorable, and right, and pure, and lovely, and admirable. Think about things that are excellent and worthy of praise."[21]
- "Don't worry about anything; instead, pray about everything."[22]

God gave us authority over our hearts:
- "Don't let your hearts be troubled. Trust in God, and trust also in me."[23]
- "Guard your heart above all else, for it determines the course of your life."[24]

God gave us authority over the enemy:
- "Look, I have given you authority over all the power of

the enemy, and you can walk among snakes and scorpions and crush them. Nothing will injure you."[25]

- "If your enemies are hungry, feed them. If they are thirsty, give them something to drink. In doing this, you will heap burning coals of shame on their heads. Don't let evil conquer you, but conquer evil by doing good."[26]

We have been given authority. Our tendency is to think a person who has authority must oversee a business, or a ministry, or a squadron. But it never begins that big. One of the problems in understanding authority is realizing that it starts so small: you have jurisdiction over *you*.

Whether you accept it or not.

The chaos in a lot of our lives stems from the vacancy of a critical position of authority, and *we* are the ones who abdicated it. We left our place in the chain of command. God, our superior, continues to give us marching orders from His Word, but we have stopped passing them down to everything under us. Someone was supposed to tell our bodies what to do, but our appetites and desires rule us like kings. Someone was supposed to tell our minds what to think, but we accept titles such as *ADHD*, and *OCD*, and *anxiety*, and the enemy takes possession of our attention because we handed him the "title" to it. Someone was supposed to tell our hearts what to feel, but we act like we cannot do anything about attractions or desires. "I can't help the way I feel," we say.

We repeat all of this out loud over and over again. And we have already discussed how powerful it is to repeat words out loud.

The excuses we speak are the "little guys," but somehow they have become the governing board, and they have hired Fear as the new CEO. Someone was supposed to tell the enemy where he could and could not go, and it was us. Now he is in a thousand places he should never have been. If he has been sitting in your chair, behind your desk, running the family business, then it is time to take back the corporation of YOU.

If your spirit, empowered by the authority of Jesus, does not tell your body and soul how things should be, then the enemy will take up the authority you have abandoned, and your life will deteriorate.

It is critical to pay attention to the way Jesus took authority: with His mouth. However, please note that when He spoke, He used well-chosen words, not volume. You may have experienced several prayer settings where believers exercised their spiritual authority over the enemy while getting louder. Most of the time, I see people feeling as if they must use volume, raising their voices and or even shouting things like, "Satan, you must shut up and get out of here!" This was not Jesus's primary method.

This is what the Father said of Jesus:

Look well at my handpicked servant;
   I love him so much, take such delight in him.
I've placed my Spirit on him;
   he'll decree justice to the nations.
But he won't yell, won't raise his voice;
   there'll be no commotion in the streets.[27]

This is how onlookers reacted to Jesus: "Everyone spoke well of him and was amazed by the gracious words that came from his lips."[28]

Even when He cast out demons, people remarked on Jesus's ability to deliver, not on His delivery. His authority was evident in

His words, not in His volume. Observers wondered aloud, "What authority and power this man's words possess! Even evil spirits obey him, and they flee at his command!"[29]

Sure, Jesus had told the demon to be quiet. But the Word says that He did not "shout or raise his voice in public."[30] So He must have done it with decorum.

Let's take a close look at two women who took authority over what they had been given without raising their voices . . . or saying anything at all.

Let's read about the first woman in Mark 12:41–44 (MSG, emphasis mine):

> Sitting across from the offering box, [Jesus] was observing how the crowd tossed money in for the collection. Many of the rich were making large contributions. One poor widow came up and put in two small coins—a measly two cents. Jesus called his disciples over and said, "The truth is that this poor widow gave more to the collection than all the others put together. All the others gave what they'll never miss; *she gave extravagantly what she couldn't afford—she gave her all.*"

The NIV says, "They all gave out of their wealth; but she, out of her poverty, put in everything—*all she had to live on.*"

And let's read about the second woman in Mark 14:3–8 (emphasis mine):

> While [Jesus] was in Bethany, reclining at the table in the home of Simon the Leper, a woman came with an alabaster jar of very expensive perfume, made of pure nard. She broke the jar and poured the perfume on his head.

Some of those present were saying indignantly to one another, "Why this waste of perfume? It could have been sold for more than a year's wages and the money given to the poor." And they rebuked her harshly.

"*Leave her alone*," said Jesus. "Why are you bothering her? She has done a beautiful thing to me. The poor you will always have with you, and you can help them any time you want. But you will not always have me. *She did what she could*."

The stunning thing about these two passages is that they are mirror images of one another. The first woman gave a couple of cents; the second gave perfume that cost a year's wages. The first gave out of her poverty; the second gave out of her wealth. But both women gave all they could give. Jesus looked upon both of them with appreciation. He saw the intention of their hearts and spoke well of them. He recognized that they had taken authority over what they had been given—in one case a little, and in the other a lot. The widow did not say that she couldn't tithe because she only had enough to live on. She didn't even say she couldn't tithe because you can't give ten percent of two cents! She didn't bother to tithe, actually. She gave one hundred percent. Stewarding what you have shows a keen understanding of authority. She gave everything to the One she knew would provide for her. And we are not given the details of how He did, but we can be sure that He did.

In the story of the second woman, however, we *are* given a glimpse into what happened after she gave. And it brings us full circle, back around to our exploration of the armor of God.

"Leave her alone," Jesus said when the religious bullies questioned her actions and her motives in giving.

She gave everything to the One she knew would protect her. He is the Word made flesh, and she knew Him personally, so she was safe. It is clear that the woman with the alabaster jar was wearing the full armor of God, even though she had never uttered a word from Ephesians 6, which hadn't even been written yet.

Her protection didn't come from committing a verse to memory; it came from committing her life to Jesus.

Our authority, power, provision, and protection don't come by knowing the words.

They come by knowing *the* Word.

The Sixth Day, Afternoon

Then God said, "Let us make human beings in our image,
to be like us. They will reign over the fish in the sea, the birds
in the sky, the livestock, all the wild animals on the earth,
and the small animals that scurry along the ground."
So God created human beings in his own image. In the image
of God he created them; male and female he created them.
Then God blessed them and said, "Be fruitful and multiply.
Fill the earth and govern it.
Reign over the fish in the sea, the birds in the sky,
and all the animals that scurry along the ground."
Then God said, "Look! I have given you every seed-bearing
plant throughout the earth and all the fruit trees for your food.
And I have given every green plant as food for all the wild
animals, the birds in the sky, and the small animals that scurry
along the ground—everything that has life." And that is what
happened. Then God looked over all he had made,
and he saw that it was very good! And evening passed
and morning came, marking the sixth day.

—

GENESIS 1:26–31 NLT

Filling His fingers with dust, Jesus stops to think. Then He spits into His palm, making mud. Dirt does not hold together on its own. Later, He will come to earth and heal a blind man by making mud with His saliva and putting it on the man's eyes.[1] This will shock everyone who witnesses such a bizarre method of healing, and He will do it to point back to this moment in the Garden.

Man is His favorite project so far. He fashions mountains of biceps and pectorals, sharpens elbows and shoulder blades. He carves a shallow valley at the throat, raking ruts and ridges into backbone. He smooths the sloping pillars of the man's legs and arms, working fingers and toes into what would eventually move as the Spirit's hands and feet in the world. He forms the lips that will speak His words.

God opens Adam's eyes like shutters, pinches his nose into place, and then . . . He breathes His breath into the man's nostrils.

"Let us make human beings in our image, to be like us," He says.

On Day Six, God gives life to mankind.

The crown of creation is finally here.

FIFTEEN

Let Them Be Made in My Image

THE PERFECTION OF CREATED THINGS, what God called "very good," did not come until He breathed life into us. We are His treasure, His precious possession. He made us in His image, destined to live according to our lineage.

Has it ever crossed your mind that the children of God don't always look related in temperament? It could be because not everyone knows what it means to be His child. But there is a coming day when the whole universe will see us in the fullness of our identity, "for all creation is waiting eagerly for that future day when God will reveal who his children really are."[2]

I don't think this is saying that God will reveal who is a Christian and who is not. I think it is saying that God will uncover our powerful relationship as His children. We are His heirs. For now, that is veiled to the world. For now, we make mistakes and missteps because sometimes we do not see who we really are either.

What do we do right now? How can we live from a lineage

that we cannot sense on some days? God did not expect humans to figure out how to live as His children. He sent His own Son, our older Brother, as an example. For Dallas Willard, this means "as a disciple I am learning from Jesus to live my life as he would live my life if he were I."[3]

Though we cannot flawlessly live our lives as Jesus would live them, we can make an attempt.

When I taught English, sometimes students would complain if they didn't feel they could successfully accomplish the skill I had asked them to practice.

"I can't!" they'd whine.

"Make an attempt," I'd answer with a smile.

"But I don't know what I'm doing!"

"Make an attempt."

"But I can't think of anything to write about!"

"Make an attempt."

I would say this over and over, always cheerfully. I used it as another one of those push-button phrases that help me communicate what is most important to me. Teachers know that most of the time these complaints from students are just excuses. When someone is making excuses, there is not a solution that will satisfy them. What is effective is getting directly to the point and then repeating the point.

I didn't make up that strategy on my own. I got it from Jesus's instructional methods. The Word says, "The LORD of Heaven's Armies is a wonderful teacher."[4] We do well to imitate Him.

Or at least to make an attempt.

When we do not live as Jesus would, then we must bring our failed attempts to light through confession—or verbally agreeing with God—that we did not act according to who we really are.

Recently, a friend shared an endearing confession that her twelve-year-old son made to her. He had disobeyed, doing something that she'd given him clear instructions not to do several times. Later, his secret disobedience nagged at him. There was tension in his tender heart, and his conscience would not let him off the hook. Finally, he came to her and said, "God has been itching me to tell you something," and he proceeded to confess.

She laughed as she told me about it. "He said, 'God has been *itching* me. I think he meant 'God has been *convicting* me.'"

The more I thought about it, the more *itching* seemed like the better word. Humans cannot scratch the surface of the sin problem. Why don't we get that by now?

Sin is a disruption to our spirits, the way a gash is a disruption to our bodies. Wounds need treatment, or infection sets in and becomes more difficult to address. You can't just hide a wound under a shirtsleeve. Wounds left untreated cause deeper pain and deeper scarring. If the infection gets bad enough, you could even lose the whole arm. In the same way, sin needs treatment, or infection sets in and it becomes more difficult to address. Sin left untreated leads to deeper pain and deeper scarring. If the infection becomes bad enough, you could even lose something that can't be recovered.

If we confess and address the problem the moment we feel God itching us, we can avoid the complications of recovery. Instead, we scratch the itch in various ways, sometimes for years.

Stop scratching, friend. God's itch won't go away.

King David would tell you the same thing. You know the story: David takes a woman into his bed while her husband, Uriah, is deployed. Immediately, David feels terrible. He knows he shouldn't have done it, and he probably swears that will be the only time it will happen. No one would have to know. But before he realizes it, the problem starts growing, because that's the nature of sin. Left untreated, infection sets in.

Bathsheba drops a bombshell: she's pregnant. And David hides the wound of his sin under his shirtsleeve. His "foolproof" plan is to call Uriah back from the battlefield and let him have some R & R at home, and then he will think the baby is his. But it doesn't happen that way. Uriah is five times the soldier David thinks he is. He chooses to sleep on the palace steps and refuses to go to his own bed while his men are still fighting in the field.

Still, David doesn't deal with the problem. He scratches the itch again. He sends Uriah back into the battle, and David gives a special order to the Israelite commander, his fierce nephew, Joab.

"Put Uriah on the frontline," he tells him. "Then pull back."

Joab gets the picture. If he follows his orders, he will become an accomplice to murder. It won't be the last time Joab has to do some dirty work his royal uncle should have been doing himself.

Or *shouldn't* have been doing himself.

Oh, David, why did you keep scratching the itch? When there is discomfort in our spirits, it is because God wants us to seek treatment, and that treatment can be found in the community of believers. If David had confessed his sin to one other person with the intention to pursue healing, things could have ended a little better. It's rarely one act of sin itself that causes total destruction. It's letting sin go untreated. Since the first acts of Creation, God has placed in us an environment that fosters life. So *everything* grows.

As you know, Uriah dies. Later David and Bathsheba's infant son dies as a consequence of their long unrepentant sin. David pens Psalm 51 as a response when God sends the prophet Nathan to confront David and get him to do what he should have done in the first place: confess.

He confesses the adultery.

He confesses the murder.

And finally his healing can begin.

I gotta tell you, I love David. He was tough enough to kill a lion and a bear with his bare hands and tender enough to sing some of the sweetest songs ever written. He is a man through and through, full of flaws and also full of greatness. God saw David's heart and said it was good. That's hard for some people to swallow, usually women. I was talking with someone once who said she just couldn't stand David. The adultery and the murder—his choices were just too much of a disappointment to her. You know, people mention the adultery and the murder, but I have never heard anyone mention the identity theft, and that is the thing that bothers *me* the most.

Have you considered the identity theft here? Have you thought about the way this story almost worked out? David's first plan was to bring Uriah home from the battlefield to be with his wife, then he would think the baby was his. But that baby wasn't born of a soldier; he was conceived by a king. David didn't care if his child grew up never knowing he was a prince. He didn't mind that his son would live in a normal neighborhood when he belonged in a palace. He was not bothered that his son would not know his true name. He was not concerned that his son would not receive his vast inheritance.

To protect his own reputation, David was willing to rob his son of his identity. He was willing to take away his legacy.

This scenario is disturbing.

"How could you do that to your child?" I want to say to David.

One day I was wondering where David would get an idea like recklessly disregarding his offspring and realized that it had happened to him too. When the prophet Samuel came to Jesse to anoint one of his sons as the next king of Israel, Jesse presented seven of his sons before Samuel, but he had *eight* sons. David, the youngest, was left out completely. Jesse didn't mention David until Samuel asked him if he had any more sons. And it wasn't just because the sheep needed tending. Later, when David went to fight Goliath, he left the sheep with a substitute shepherd. It could have been done in this case too.

It's a good thing Jesse wasn't calling the shots for David's life. He didn't exactly recognize his son's destiny and identity, but thankfully, God has the last word for His children.

"Man looks at the outward appearance," God said of David, "but the Lord looks at the heart. . . . I have found . . . a man after My own heart."[5]

As the son of the High King of Heaven, David inherited a royal legacy.

Jesse really had no idea what was going to happen through his lineage. The regal roots of his family tree were only *beginning* with David, and he couldn't see it. How could God have explained that much later, from the line of Jesse, there would come another, greater descendant? Not just a king, but the King of kings: Jesus.

Jesse didn't even know who *he* really was. As a result, he did not see his son for who he was.

But what Jesse did not see in himself or call out in his son, God did.

And God's Word stood.

Your identity comes from God, your heavenly Father, and no earthly father can interfere. God, your Maker, can restore you to truth any time you have neglected to live as who (and Whose) you are.

That is what sin really is: neglecting to live as who (and Whose) we are.

Legacy is important to God. He designed us to pass on our inheritance to those coming after us. The way we do so is by giving ourselves fully to Whom we belong.

Jesus brilliantly emphasizes this in the book of Matthew. Some teachers of the law try to trap Him by asking whether it is right to pay taxes. Jesus makes a profound sermon illustration by pointing to a coin, stamped with the image of Caesar.

"Give to Caesar what belongs to Caesar," He says, "and *give to God what belongs to God.*"

Give your tax to the government, He is saying, but give your life to God.

His image is stamped on *you*.[6]

The other day my five-year-old nephew scooted up to my brother and said, "I love sitting close to my real fake father."

"Your *what*?" my brother asked.

"You are my real fake father," my nephew answered, "because God is my real Father."

Okay, he may not have had the right terminology at such a young age, but he had his theology straight.

You and I do not get our identity from our earthly fathers, no matter how bad or how good they have been. The role of an earthly father is important beyond what we can fathom, but our identity comes from our heavenly Father.

And what does our identity have to do with confession? Everything! Confession is verbally agreeing with what God has said about us. Confession is returning to our true selves in Christ. In Psalm 51:10, David writes, "Create in me a pure heart, O God, and renew a steadfast spirit within me."

David was created with a clean heart and a right spirit. That was his identity. When God saw a king within that shepherd in the field, it was because He saw a man with a heart like His. God's heart was supposed to be David's legacy, passed down to all those who would be born after him. By covering up his sin, David was trying to live with a wounded heart, which he was never meant to do. He needed confession because he needed to heal and return to who God had created him to be.

When I imagine what would have happened if David's son had grown up as Uriah's son, I shudder. What would he have felt upon hearing the truth as a grown man? He would have looked back upon all the years that he'd lived without what was rightfully his, and he would have become bitter toward his biological father.

The same thing can happen to us. We are made in God's image, and we are children of the King. God's heart is the legacy we are supposed to bestow to future generations. Our spiritual inheritance is rich and sweet; we have plenty to pass down. But when we do not recognize it, we live in spiritual poverty and become bitter toward our real Father. Our hearts ache from dreams never realized, when actually, the only thing we never realized was who we really were.

Bitterness is a legacy too. If we're not careful, we'll pass it down.

There is a way to make bitter hearts sweet again.

In Exodus 15, the Israelites have left Egypt, making it through the Red Sea, and they are not in the desert long before they ache with thirst. They find a pool of water at a place called Marah, but it is bitter, and they cannot drink it. The people cry out to the Lord, and He shows Moses a branch, telling him to throw it in the water. When the branch hits the pool, the water becomes sweet, and the people are nourished by clean water.

Many times in the Bible our hearts are referred to as water. In Lamentations, we are told to pour our hearts out like water in the presence of the Lord.[7] In Proverbs, we read we are to guard our hearts because they are the deep wellspring from which our lives flow forth.[8]

Sin makes the water of our hearts as bitter and ineffective in the Kingdom as the pool of undrinkable water was to the Israelites. But when we cry out to the Lord as David did, "Create in me a clean heart, O God. Renew a loyal spirit within me,"[9] we are reaching out to the One who can make bitter water sweet, the One who can make stagnant water clean.

And how does He do it?

God showed Moses a branch and told him to apply it to the bitter water.

He does the same for us.

Isaiah 11:1 says, "A shoot will come up from the stump of Jesse; from his roots a Branch will bear fruit." The word *Branch* is capitalized, and what follows is a description of the ministry of Jesus.

God has shown us a Branch. When we apply the Branch to our bitter hearts, they become sweet again.

We want to leave a legacy that is better, not bitter.

And what about those who would like to break off from the bitter legacy they have received? Even if circumstances have left your heart feeling as hard as a rock, Christ offers a solution.

In the description of Jesus's ministry, something stands out, especially in light of the next story of Moses in Exodus. Just two chapters later, the Israelite community is thirsty again, and Moses cries out for a solution, and God tells him, "Strike the rock, and water will come gushing out."[10] It happened just as the Lord said.

Do you think it is a coincidence that right after Isaiah writes that a Branch will come from Jesse, he writes of Him, "He will strike the earth with the rod of his mouth; with the breath of his lips he will slay the wicked"?[11]

Jesus wants fresh, sweet, nourishing water to pour forth from every heart on this earth. One way He accomplishes this is through the application of Himself to our hearts. The other way is by striking the earth with the rod of His mouth.

The Word of God is not just a book. It causes life to flow in us.

Jesus extends an irresistible invitation: "Anyone who believes in me may come and drink! For the Scriptures declare, 'Rivers of living water will flow from his heart.'"[12]

God's gift to us is new life.

We must see ourselves and our identity through inward rather than outward mirrors. We do not draw our worth from careers or achievements or family life or skills or talents. None of these have anything to do with who we are. If we want to know who we really are, we should hide God's Word in our hearts.[13]

"But," James urges us, "don't just listen to God's word. You must do what it says. Otherwise, you are only fooling yourselves. For if you listen to the word and don't obey, it is like glancing at your face in a mirror. You see yourself, walk away, and forget what you look like. But if you look carefully into the perfect law that sets you free, and if you do what it says and don't forget what you heard, then God will bless you for doing it."[14]

When was the last time you read the blessing that comes to those who obey?

It is so expansive and beautiful, I have been waiting excitedly for the day we would write it down and begin saying it over ourselves.

Let There Be Legacy
(from Deuteronomy 28:1–13)

I know that if I, _____, fully obey the Lord my God and carefully follow all His commands, the Lord my God will set me high above all the nations on Earth. All these blessings will come on me and accompany me if I obey the Lord my God: I will be blessed in the city and blessed in the country. My children will be blessed, and my finances will be blessed. My home will be blessed. I will be blessed when I come in and blessed when I go out.

The Lord will grant that the enemies who rise up against me will be defeated before me. They will come at me from one direction but flee from me in seven.

The Lord will send a blessing on everything I own and on everything I put my hand to. The Lord my God will bless me in everything He gives me.

The Lord will establish me as His legacy, as He promised me on oath, if I keep the commands of the Lord my God and walk in obedience to Him. Then all the peoples on earth will see that I am called by the name of the Lord, and they will fear me. The Lord will grant me abundant prosperity in all things.

The Lord will open the heavens, the storehouse of his bounty, to send rain on my land in season and to bless all the work of my hands. I will lend to many but will borrow from none. The Lord will make me the head, not the tail. If I pay attention to the commands of the Lord and carefully follow them, I will always be at the top, never at the bottom.

Isn't it clear that God could not have given all of this to us until this stage in the divine sequence of re-creation? Before we could receive an inheritance like this one, we had to be people who would know what to do with it. We had to have revelation and wisdom first. We had to be completely free to believe and receive. We had to know our purpose as His children and begin living productively. We had to trust God's guidance and know where we are going. We had to be strengthened by community and confident of our authority. Only then could we receive our legacy without squandering it like the prodigal son. We had to learn to hold on to it if we were going to pass it down.

God made us in His image. We carry His DNA. But if we do not look into the Word, hidden in our hearts, then we will not see ourselves for who we really are and we will not follow His commands. No wonder we struggle to think as our Father thinks and do as He does.

Every good gift and every perfect gift is from above, and comes down from the Father of lights, with whom there is no variation or shadow of turning. Of His own will He brought us forth by the word of truth, that we might be a kind of firstfruits of His creatures.[15]

He is the Father of lights and we are "children of the light."[16] Therefore, the more we look *to* Him, the more we look *like* Him, for "those who look to him for help will be radiant with joy."[17]

May it be said of us:

They did not conquer the land with their swords;
    it was not their own strong arm that gave them victory.
It was your right hand and strong arm
    and *the blinding light from your face that helped them,*
    for you loved them.[18]

With our Father's help, we can resist overpowering temptation and recover from the destruction of sin to be restored as King David was. We have everything we need, but it does not come from ourselves. Victory is our inheritance. It comes from God. Our children need us to take hold of what is ours so that we can pass it on to them.

The only legacy we can leave is one we have received.

SIXTEEN

Legacy

MY NEPHEW IS CAREFREE. He is a wonderful jumble of life. He enjoys every day and is in constant play mode. He doesn't worry about much of anything.

The other day we were playing in the front yard while I was babysitting. His mother came back from her errand, and she rolled down the window as she was pulling up in the driveway. She reminded him to stay in the grass until she parked. He obeyed, but the instant her van pulled into the garage, he took off running faster than I could grab him. Her taillights were still on, and I saw the van rock backward at the same time he reached the bumper area.

"No! Come back now!" I screamed with such force, my voice dropped an octave. I was frightened, but I sounded more angry than afraid.

He turned and came back to me, his chin quivering.

"I just wanted . . ." He swallowed hard. "I just wanted to get to my toys in the garage."

Oh, the massive tears in his eyes.

"I know, I know! You didn't do anything wrong, but it's not

safe to go behind the car until your mom gets out. She can't see you back there. You scared me. I don't want you to be hurt."

Is there any possible way, when my nephew has never driven a car, that he can understand that the driver cannot see him? Even though I tried to explain it in simple terms, he kept holding back a full-on cry. He never understood the impending danger. All he knew was that I had raised my voice at him when he hadn't been doing anything wrong.

All he understood was the hurt.

Even God's efforts to protect us can feel like He is disciplining us when we have done nothing wrong. All we understand is the hurt.

If only we knew how much more it would hurt if He *didn't* look out for us. Maybe we need to stop focusing on what He is prohibiting and trust that He is protecting.

Think of a stoplight. When a traffic signal changes to red, it has no desire to thwart you. It is not asking you to stop for any reason other than to protect you and other drivers. But if you are in a rush, you may feel like the lights are out to get you. They seem to have made it personal. Haven't you almost thought that before? The later you are for an appointment, the more it hurts when you hit a red light. But it would hurt a lot more if you hit a car. So you submit to the signal, knowing you can't see ahead clearly.

We can submit to God as well. We know we can't see ahead clearly. There is so much out there that we cannot anticipate. Most of the time we don't even know to be afraid.

God tells us we do not have to be.

Fear the LORD, you his godly people,
  for those who fear him will have all they need.

Even strong young lions sometimes go hungry,

   but those who trust in the LORD will lack no good
thing.[19]

We couldn't see or understand the dangers around us even if He explained them in the simplest terms. We do not know how much He is protecting us until we push past His protection. And sometimes when we feel safe, we are in the most danger. The only secure option we will ever have is to depend upon our Creator. When life appears to be at its darkest, we fear that we are outside God's loving care. The truth is that we never leave the protection of His hands.

In fact, the more He closes His hands over us in protection, the darker it can seem.

Humans are not naturally fearless. Everyone faces fear. But Christians should take action when they experience fear, submitting their general, unhealthy fear to the character-building, healthy fear of the Lord. They know that "perfect love expels all fear. If we are afraid, it is for fear of punishment, and this shows that we have not fully experienced his perfect love."[20] Our loving Father may use adversity to correct and redirect us, but He won't use it to punish us because Jesus has already taken punishment in our place. To perceive trials as "your punishment" is to suggest that Jesus did not take it all, and that there is a little more punishment that you must bear in addition to what He already has borne. Such an attitude may seem humble, but it is dangerously prideful.

Fear the Lord. Do not fear punishment.

Also, do not fear the enemy. If you give much thought to Satan, you may be afraid of him, but that would also be a mistake. He is not all-powerful. He is not on an equal plane with God. The two are not opposites. God is uncreated. He has no beginning. No hand formed Him. Satan is created. He has a beginning, and the hand that formed him was God's. Satan was made for wonderful Kingdom purposes by the same Creator who made us. Lucifer has abandoned the good works that were designed for him, and there has been much havoc in the wake of that decision. But he cannot operate without God's permission.

Fearing the Lord means fearing what life would look like without Him. It means fearing to take one step out from under His protection. It means fearing His displeasure more than our fellow man's.

Fear of the Lord can be called the One Fear. Because the man who fears the Lord doesn't have to fear anything else. How do we fear the Lord?

> Come, my children, and listen to me,
>   and I will teach you to fear the LORD.
> Does anyone want to live a life
>   that is long and prosperous?
> Then keep your tongue from speaking evil
>   and your lips from telling lies![21]

You might be tempted to say, "But I am a good person. I don't speak evil. And I don't have a problem with lying." Even that statement is out of alignment with God's Word. Jesus Himself said, "Why do you call me good? No one is good—except God alone."[22]

As we have examined, our words have tremendous power. With our words we either agree or disagree with God about our lives. The enemy is constantly telling us lies about every aspect of ourselves as new creations.

He tells us that we are not capable of *revelation*.

He tells us that we do not deserve to be *free*.

He tells us that we do not have a *purpose*.

He tells us that we will never be *productive*.

He tells us that God is still not giving us *guidance*.

He tells us that we do not need *community*.

He tells us that we do not have power or *authority*.

He tells us that we are worthless and have nothing to leave as a *legacy*.

If any of these lies have entered your thoughts as you have been reading this book, it is Satan trying to trick you to keep you from living as a new creation. Becoming a new creation is not a choice. It *has already happened to you* if you have surrendered your life to Christ Jesus. But you do have a choice about whether you live as if it is true.

To tell any other story about yourself is to lie. If we are speaking evil to ourselves, about ourselves, then of course our lives will be short and miserable. We are not fearing the Lord enough to believe what He has said and done.

Fear of the Lord is submission to Him and to what He says . . . about us.

The spiritual discipline of submission is probably the most difficult of all. This is what the Bible says about submission:

- "Submit yourselves therefore to God."[23]
- "But I want you to realize that the head of every man is Christ, and the head of the woman is man, and the head of Christ is God."[24]
- "Submit to one another out of reverence for Christ."[25]
- "Submit yourselves for the Lord's sake to every human authority."[26]
- "Obey your leaders and submit to them, for they are

keeping watch over your souls, as those who will have to give an account."[27]

- "In the same way, you who are younger, submit yourselves to your elders."[28]
- "Now as the church submits to Christ, so also wives should submit in everything to their husbands."[29]
- "The women should keep silent in the churches. For they are not permitted to speak, but should be in submission, as the Law also says."[30]

That last one is why I will not teach in doctrinal leadership positions or participate in governance decisions within the church. There is no question that this is difficult for some women. Submission is a spiritual discipline. Disciplines are things we would not naturally do on our own. They take concentrated effort, but when applied regularly, they completely change us. To deliberately choose submission will transform you into the likeness of Christ like nothing else. If we want to be like Him, we must submit. There are many times when Jesus showed us the discipline of submission in His life. I will summarize all of them by offering one:

Don't you believe that I am in the Father, and that the Father is in me? The words I say to you I do not speak on my own authority. Rather, *it is the Father, living in me, who is doing his work.*[31]

Even Jesus didn't speak on His own. He submitted to His Father, who was living within Him. Jesus is illustrating for us what life in the Spirit looks like. The Word says that "it is God *who works in [us]* to will and to act in order to fulfill his good purpose."[32]

We belong to God, and now we must submit to Him. Submission isn't slavery; it is family. The Bible explains that our legacy as family members will have responsibilities:

> And since we are his children, we are his heirs. In fact, together with Christ we are heirs of God's glory. But if we are to share his glory, we must also share his suffering.[33]

We are children! Heirs of heaven! It sounds exciting. But if you are anything like me, you often want the benefits of belonging to God without the responsibilities. Did you read that last sentence of the scripture above? We're told that if we are to share in Jesus's glory, we must share in His suffering. What comes to mind when I think of Christ's suffering is not the last hours on the cross. It is the moment in the Garden of Gethsemane when Jesus cried and sweat drops of blood. He was already bleeding, even before He was beaten. He was already suffering, even before He felt one lash of the whip. What brought Him to that point of heart-crushing agony?

Submission.

He did not pursue His will: that the painful cup of crucifixion pass Him by.

Instead, He accepted His Father's will: that He, the sinless One, would die a sinner's death in our place.

Submission hurts sometimes. Everything, everything, everything in my life is put into proper perspective when I envision Jesus submitting to the point of sweating blood. There are times I work hard to submit to God's will instead of my own, but I have to admit I have never worked *that* hard. None of us has. Hebrews 12:4 says, "In your struggle against sin, you have not yet resisted to the point of shedding your blood."

The other day I was talking to a friend in a coffee shop, and when a sore subject from the past came up, I felt accused. Suddenly I found myself blurting out a defensive response about that past event. I wasn't angry at her; I was angry about the situation. Without thinking, I muttered a curse word in frustration.

I left our meeting in a state of conviction. When I was much younger I would say curse words here and there, almost to be humorous. It seemed funny that a "good girl" would occasionally curse. But God is clear on even this small point, which is not as small as we think. The Bible tells us, "Do not let any unwholesome talk come out of your mouths, but only what is helpful for building others up according to their needs, that it may benefit those who listen."[34]

I cannot overstate how much God cares about what we say.

Jesus has commissioned me to use my words to teach through writing and speaking. Do I expect Him to have no opinion when I use my words to bless and also use my words to curse? Our words have much more power than that.

"Can both fresh water and salt water flow from the same spring?"[35] the Bible asks.

In 1818, William Law was concerned about the number of Christians who thought they were living pious or God-fearing lifestyles but still made it a practice to use curse words. He determined that their problem was they were focused on maintaining religiosity, not maintaining relationship, which requires intention.

The reason of common swearing is this: It is because men have not so much as the intention to please God in all their actions. For let a man but have so much piety as to intend to please God in all the actions of his life, as the happiest and best thing in the world, and then he will never swear more. It will be as impossible for him to swear, whilst he feels this intention within himself, as it is impossible for a man that intends to please his Prince, to go up and abuse him to his face.[36]

Because I want to maintain my close relationship with Christ more than I want to maintain my schedule, I drove right to the park from that coffee date with my friend and submitted in humility. I put aside what was next on my to-do list in order to sit at His feet. I asked the Lord why I had used that curse word. He revealed that I had a deep, deep well of anger related to the topic we had been discussing. That well was filled to brimming. I had used a curse word that day because "out of the abundance of the heart [the] mouth speaks."[37]

There was no way to maintain my schedule *or* my composure then. I prayed about my anger until my emotions started pouring out of me in tearful rage. I was crying and praying and feeling furious at the same time. That deep well of anger was actually a volcano. After an hour of prayer, all of the old bitterness had erupted, and I had allowed God to heal me of my past. But I never would have seen the volcano or dealt with it in time if I had not submitted my speech for God's inspection.

Even *one* misspoken word matters.

Through the act of submitting my speech, I was not enslaved but set free. I deeply value the call God has placed on my life. I want to use my words to lead people to freedom, but I cannot do that if I am in a prison myself.

I cannot pass on a legacy I do not possess.

A biblical hero of mine is Moses, who had a rocky road of submitting his words to God. At first, he didn't feel qualified to speak on behalf of God. They had a couple of arguments about that, during which—pay close attention here!—Moses did not keep his tongue from evil and his lips from speaking lies.

He said to God, "Pardon your servant, Lord. I have never been eloquent, neither in the past nor since you have spoken to your servant. *I am slow of speech and tongue.*"[38]

That was a lie.

In Acts 7:22, we learn that, lo and behold, "Moses was educated in all the wisdom of the Egyptians and was *powerful in speech and action*" (emphasis mine).

How in the world do you go from the truth that you are *powerful in speech* to saying out loud that you are *slow of speech*? Well, that verse we read in Psalm 34 says that it happens when we do not live in fear of the Lord, which would mean that we are submitting to His voice and not the enemy's. Moses would have to learn to submit his speech to God over and over again as he walked out his calling as a leader to freedom. Ultimately, it was said of Moses that his faith was exercised through *submission*. In the famous chronicle of faith in Hebrews 11, we see his motivation.

> It was by faith that Moses, when he grew up, refused to be called the son of Pharaoh's daughter. He chose to share the oppression of God's people instead of enjoying the fleeting pleasures of sin. He thought it was better to suffer *for the sake of Christ* than to own the treasures of Egypt, for he was looking ahead to his great reward.[39]

Moses chose to submit and suffer for the sake of Christ. That was his motivation.

What?! Way back in the Old Testament, Moses did what he did for Jesus! If Moses didn't even *know* Jesus and made an attempt to submit to Him, how much more should we submit? We not only know Christ, but have Him living within us.

Moses had the best life the world could offer at the time. He was an heir of Pharaoh and stood to inherit the treasures of Egypt. But he did not consider equality with Pharaoh something to hold on to. He chose a different legacy.

This is the pattern of one who wants to be transformed into the likeness of Christ.

You and I can pursue the same attitude that Christ Jesus had.

Though he was God,
> *he did not think of equality with God*
> *as something to cling to.*
Instead, he gave up his divine privileges;
> he took the humble position of a slave
> and was born as a human being.
When he appeared in human form,
> he humbled himself in obedience to God
> and died a criminal's death on a cross.

Therefore, God elevated him to the place of highest honor
> and gave him the name above all other names,
that at the name of Jesus every knee should bow,
> in heaven and on earth and under the earth,
and every tongue declare that Jesus Christ is Lord,
> to the glory of God the Father.[40]

The One who created humans did not resist when they captured Him.

While humans were beating His back, He kept their hearts beating.

He let humans take away His final breath, so that He could breathe the Holy Spirit into them.

Jesus submitted, humbling Himself and putting Himself under His Father. Then He submitted to human authorities. The result of Jesus's submission to men was that God inverted the order and set Him higher than any other. Therefore, when we are under Christ, we are in line to receive everything that belongs to Him.

A holy legacy is ready to pour out.

All we have to do is put ourselves under the flow.

The Seventh Day

So the creation of the heavens and the earth
and everything in them was completed.
On the seventh day God had finished his work
of creation, so he rested from all his work.
And God blessed the seventh day and declared it holy,
because it was the day when he rested
from all his work of creation. This is the account
of the creation of the heavens and the earth.

—

GENESIS 2:1–4 NLT

The Creator looks upon the earth, and with satisfaction, He declares that all of it is very good. Then the One who crafted time honors what He has made by taking time for Himself. God's rest doesn't look like doing nothing. It looks like enjoying. He knows how to rest well: with eyes and ears open, with heart and mind still.

Jesus walks in the Garden in the cool of the day.[1] He meanders under the shadows of tamarinds and date palms, tasting their sugared goodness. Leaning against a stone, He dips His feet into the Tigris River. The water ripples at His ankles.

He reaches for a bit of honeycomb. Admires a hawk in flight. Laughs as an ant tries to lift the leaf from a fig. He stands still in a jasmine breeze. Makes His knuckle a perch for a finch.

He ruffles the mane of a lion. Touches the velvet back of a lamb's ear.

He sighs as the sunset sky spreads from honey to blood.

"It is finished," Jesus says for the first time. And all creation begins waiting for the moment He will say it again.

On Day Seven, God rested.

SEVENTEEN

God Rested

WHY DID THE GOD WHO never slumbers nor sleeps[2] need to rest? Why did He stop work in order to appreciate His work? It seems obvious to me now.

God didn't need it; He chose it.

In the book of Ecclesiates, Solomon observed that there is a time, or season, for everything:

a time to be born and a time to die,
a time to plant and a time to uproot,
a time to kill and a time to heal,
a time to tear down and a time to build,
a time to weep and a time to laugh,
a time to mourn and a time to dance,
a time to scatter stones and a time to gather them,
a time to embrace and a time to refrain from embracing,
a time to search and a time to give up,
a time to keep and a time to throw away,
a time to tear and a time to mend,
a time to be silent and a time to speak,
a time to love and a time to hate,
a time for war and a time for peace.[3]

There is a time to create. And a time to rest. There is a time to work and a time to appreciate your work.

God chose to rest, and since He never asks us to do anything that He hasn't done first, by choosing rest He was providing a conduit for relationship with us. He desires that we imitate Him, choosing rest and coming directly to Him for it. The core of every spiritual discipline is rest in God. We do not *earn* by pursuing these practices. Through these practices, we *learn* that we are being pursued by God.

He tackles us with grace. Like Jacob, we have been wrestling with Him to bless us. Oh, that we would realize much faster than Jacob: the blessing isn't in wrestling; it is in resting.

A friend of mine says that grace knocks us off our feet so that we don't have a leg to stand on before Christ. But then it gives us a backbone so that we can stand again, knowing who we are in Christ.

Grace is not about doing but *being*. The point of grace is that we don't work for it. The very definition of grace is rest.

It is heartbreaking when God says, "In repentance and rest is your salvation, in quietness and trust is your strength, but you would have none of it."[4]

God longs for us to come to Him for rest. Why will we have none of it?

If rest is the last thing we have time for, it is the main thing we need.

I remember the day I answered the phone, and a friend was crying so hard that it was difficult to understand her. Though she tried, her great anxiety prevented her from fully explaining her thoughts. She was having a panic attack. Her emotions were frayed and tangled like a mess of severed electrical wires.

In the past, I would have started looking inside myself for

answers, flipping through a catalog of comforting scriptures or book quotes in my mind. Thank goodness I have lived enough to know I don't have the answers. Now I know that I cannot possibly produce any prescription for someone who is hurting that badly. She needed to find rest in God alone. He is the One with all the answers, not me. He is the Source she needed to plug into for refreshment. My role in that moment was just to give her a chance to be with Him.

"What are you planning to do in the next couple of hours?" I asked.

"Putting the little one down for a nap, then I have to clean the house because the babysitter will be here later, then I—"

"Wait a second. Maybe you shouldn't do that. That's a lot of moving around. That's a lot of noise. What might help right now is to be still and quiet. Look, if you will let me, I can come over and watch the kids. I can straighten the house a little bit too."

"No . . . no, it's okay . . . ," she tried to protest.

"I know you will feel vulnerable, but just let me. My house is probably messier than yours anyway, so it won't bother me. It is a beautiful day, and you don't want to miss it. God is definitely speaking through nature. Have you seen how gorgeous it is outside? If you need to hear His voice, then you gotta get outside and get alone with Him. Sing praise music, read your Bible, whatever you want, but don't start making lists or plans. Just rest in His presence. Just rest."

"I . . . uh . . . All right. Come over."

When I arrived, she looked frazzled and teary. Her brow was furrowed, and she seemed at the furthest point of fatigue. She grabbed her Bible and a couple other things, maybe a book and a journal, and left hesitantly. She looked back at me and her kids a couple of times before she got into the car.

What she needed most was *to receive*, but it was hard for her to let go of what she thought she needed *to give*.

The kids and I had fun. We made a game of picking up the living room.

"Wait, when are we going to have playtime?" her four-year-old daughter asked.

"This *is* playtime!" I said, handing her a paper towel and spraying her name in foaming cleaner on the bathroom mirror.

"No, this is definitely *not* playtime, but I'll do it," she sighed.

In a half hour, we were finished and were playing mini golf outside. The whole afternoon was a pleasure for me. Not one bit of it was an inconvenience. All I could think about was how special it felt to give the gift of a holy meeting to my friend. Our precious job as servants of Christ is to make meeting places for others, to give them time and space to hear from God. There is no gift that is as meaningful to the heart. Especially when we do not have enough funds to purchase gifts for others, we can remember that the gift of *time* is priceless. It is one of those things that is free but of invaluable worth. The instant I had sensed her need to rest, I saw my chance to give my friend a little bit of time alone.

I gave her time to do the finest thing: be with God.

When she walked in the door a couple of hours later, she looked like a new person. Her face was refreshed, and she had an easy smile. She even looked younger.

"Wow. Thank you," she said. "That made all the difference. As I sat outside, I kept coming back to Psalm 66:16–20." She let me read it from her phone.

> Come and hear, all you who fear God;
>   let me tell you what he has done for me.
> I cried out to him with my mouth;

his praise was on my tongue.
If I had cherished sin in my heart,
    the Lord would not have listened;
but God has surely listened
    and has heard my prayer.
Praise be to God,
    who has not rejected my prayer
    or withheld his love from me!

"Look at how it says, 'If I had cherished sin in my heart, the Lord would not have listened.' *If I had cherished sin,* it says. I was cherishing some things that I really needed to surrender. No wonder I was having a panic attack. I *needed* this break today. I needed a chance to let go of those thoughts and listen to God about this situation. At first, I didn't want to let you help me today; I thought I could do it alone. But today reminded me how important it is to let somebody help you. Just let somebody help you."

My friend learned something that God wants all of us to learn through deliberate rest: you and I are not the ones holding it all together. He is.

[Jesus] existed before anything was created and is supreme
over all creation, for through him God created everything
    in the heavenly realms and on earth.
He made the things we can see
    and the things we can't see—
such as thrones, kingdoms, rulers, and authorities in the
unseen world.
    Everything was created through him and for him.
He existed before anything else,
    and he holds all creation together.[5]

He holds all creation together. Regular rest keeps us from holding on too tight, from trying to do Jesus's job for Him.

Rest lets go.

Even during our darkest seasons, peace can be ours, but surrender must come first. We have to let go. We cannot reach for hope if our hands are already full of other things.

In a collection of his letters entitled *Let Go*, Francois Fenelon, a French Roman Catholic archbishop who lived in the seventeenth century, writes:

> Let me tell you what real surrender is. It is simply resting in the love of God, as a little baby rests in his mother's arms. A perfect surrender must even be willing to quit surrendering, if that is what God wants! We renounce ourselves, and yet, God never lets us know when it is complete. If we knew, it would no longer be complete, for there is nothing that bolsters the ego quite so much as knowing that it is fully surrendered! . . .
>
> If we are restless and concerned about things formerly renounced, we have not genuinely surrendered. Surrender is the source of true peace; if we aren't at peace, it is because our surrender is not complete.[6]

If you need peace, then let go, get alone with God, and get some rest. Rest is available to us. There is nothing like this promise: "The Lord is near. Do not be anxious about anything, but in every situation, by prayer and petition, with thanksgiving, present your requests to God. And the peace of God, which transcends all understanding, will guard your hearts and your minds in Christ Jesus."[7]

People think of rest as something that happens to them, that they can't *choose* to rest. They think, *If my mind is racing, then how can I rest?*

God will give it to you if you allow Him. No specific action is required, but some *inaction* is:

> It is useless for you to work so hard
>   from early morning until late at night,
> anxiously working for food to eat;
>   for God gives rest to his loved ones.[8]

In other words, slow down.

Sabbath is not an option. It is one of the Ten Commandments. I have heard people ask what they are supposed to do on a Sabbath. Do whatever you do when you stop earning and start enjoying. Do what you do when you want to be refreshed and renewed. Do what God did when He rested: keep your eyes and ears open, and your heart and mind still. Laugh. Cook. Read. Run. Play. Take a trip. Take a walk. Take a break. Take a nap. Take your retirement one *day* at a time and spread it over your lifetime. Don't save it all until the end.

Rest is that simple.

But many of us think we are being victorious and resilient if we say, "I can keep going longer. I don't need to rest yet. Look! I'm not tired!" My three-year-old niece says the same thing.

That's not being a champ. It's being a child.

God's directive for Sabbath is critical, and we should take a moment to read it closely.

> Remember to observe the Sabbath day by keeping it holy.
> You have six days each week for your ordinary work, but
> the seventh day is a Sabbath day of rest dedicated to the

LORD your God. On that day no one in your household may do any work. This includes you, your sons and daughters, your male and female servants, your livestock, and any foreigners living among you. For in six days the LORD made the heavens, the earth, the sea, and everything in them; but on the seventh day he rested. That is why the LORD blessed the Sabbath day and set it apart as holy.[9]

We have been instructed to rest, and if we do not, we are being disobedient. This command is a gift. It is for our benefit. The consequences that come with disobedience will find us if we do not observe the Sabbath. Emotional, physical, and psychological problems will manifest in the life of the person who does not rest.

The next time you are frayed by stress or torn by a storm, create a quiet moment to seek Him, even if it means you have to call a friend and risk vulnerability in asking for an hour of help with the kids. These are new and freeing days when authenticity is highly prized. We hate the hypocrite and have no taste for the fake. Remind yourself that if you do not share your struggle, then you are hiding it, which is much worse than sharing it. Stop thinking that you will feel better once your house is clean. Stop thinking that your spirits will be lifted if you spend some time on social media. Stop thinking you will feel rested by relaxing in front of the television for a little while.

There's nothing wrong with these things. They help temporarily. But if you need real rest, you won't find it there.

And if a friend calls when he is burdened by depression or she is shaken by fear, then do everything you can to nudge your friend toward Jesus, which does not mean quoting from the latest church sermon or inspirational book. It means doing what you can to give that person an opportunity for time alone with Him. Sometimes it may require that you give up some of your own time, but it will end up as a blessing to both of you. Stop feeling you have to think of the perfect answer.

There is nothing more fitting than "an apt reply."[10] But if your friends need rest, they won't find it in advice.

You may need to realize that you can offer rest to someone only if you have received rest yourself. Have you? Are you deeply aware of it? Put your commitment to rest in writing, look yourself in the eye, and say it out loud today.

Let There Be Rest
(from Hebrews 4:1–11 NLT)

I, _____, know that God's promise of entering His rest still stands for me, so I ought to tremble with fear that I might fail to experience it. For this good news—that God has prepared this rest—has been announced to me just as it was to the Israelites long ago. But it did them no good because they didn't share the faith of those who listened to God. For only we who believe can enter His rest. As for the others, God said, "In my anger I took an oath: 'They will never enter my place of rest,'" even though this rest has been ready since He made the world. We know it is ready because of the place in the Scriptures where it mentions the seventh day: "On the seventh day God rested from all his work." But in the other passage God said, "They will never enter my place of rest."

So God's rest is there for people to enter, but those

---

who first heard this good news failed to enter because they disobeyed God. So God set another time for entering His rest, and that time is today. God announced this through David much later in the words already quoted: "Today when you hear his voice, don't harden your hearts."

Now if Joshua had succeeded in giving the Israelites this rest, God would not have spoken about another day of rest still to come. So there is a special rest still waiting for the people of God. For all who have entered into God's rest have rested from their labors, just as God did after creating the world. So let us do our best to enter that rest. But if we disobey God, as the people of Israel did, we will fall.

Not long ago, I was heartsore about several prayers that were unsettled in my life and struggles that had mounted in intensity. At the last minute, I decided to go to a women's conference to seek encouragement and direction from God *one more time*. I bought a ticket for a seat but didn't sit there. I just found an obscure place in the back of the auditorium, on a bench against the wall. I didn't want anyone to see me cry as much as I knew I was going to.

Later, a friend found me in the dark corner and asked me to come sit by her. She knew nothing of what was bothering me. She didn't know I was worried and that I felt I was at a breaking point. That is why I was surprised when, about halfway through the conference, she turned to me with a prophetic encouragement from God that would change my perspective on rest forever. She said, "Nika, the Lord wants you to know you are in the bow. You are an arrow, and the increasing tension you feel every day is only the tension of His hand pulling you back as He takes aim. Soon enough He will launch you, and you will finally understand that the tension you are experiencing now was only to increase how far you would fly."

That thought has returned to me again and again. Every time things get hard, I try to thank God for the increasing tension.

His timing is perfect for you. His love for you is intense. He carries every detail about the desires of your heart in His own heart. He will not forget you or what He has said to you. If you feel tension right now, it may be because you are an arrow in the bow. Submit, and let Him take aim. You are in His hands while you are in the bow. You can rest secure and stop worrying. Soon enough, He will let you fly.

To be ready to launch, the arrow must be still in the hands of the Archer.

Be still. Don't waste your time of rest in the bow by being distracted. I remember a time when my mother and I met a friend for dinner to see pictures from his trip to San Antonio. He was from Taiwan, and had only been in Texas for a year. As a native Texan, I anticipated viewing the familiar sights from his perspective. We looked through his photos excitedly, waiting to see the colorful fabric of the Mexican market, the lovely lights of the River Walk, and the scalloped silhouette of the Alamo.

What we saw instead were squirrels.

There were pictures of squirrels on sidewalks, squirrels on the sides of buildings, squirrels on park benches, and squirrels scurrying up trees. My mother and I looked at one another, thinking, *Huh?*

Our friend explained that there are no squirrels in Taiwan. He was amazed by their adorable bodies and fluffy tails. Squirrels are neat to someone who has never seen them, I guess. But to me, they are common and insignificant. So all I could think as I looked over his pictures of San Antonio that were not of San Antonio was, *Poor guy. He missed it.*

May we never miss the glorious rest of God because we are distracted by what is common and insignificant.

The Alamo is right beside you. Stop looking at the squirrels.

Jesus is asking, "Are you tired? Worn out? Burned out on religion? *Come to me. Get away with me and you'll recover your life.* I'll show you how to take a real rest. Walk with me and work with me— watch how I do it. Learn the unforced rhythms of grace. I won't lay anything heavy or ill-fitting on you. Keep company with me and you'll learn to live freely and lightly."[11]

If we need rest, there is only one place we can find it: in the hands of the One who chose to rest so that we could too.

Just be still. His faithful fingers hold the bow.

EIGHTEEN

Renewal

WE HAVE COME to the last phase, but your pursuit of new life is not over. The divine sequence of re-creation is actually a divine *cycle*. What began with revelation finally reaches renewal, which means it will begin again. God rested on the seventh day because He was about to start over.

Constant creation is His way. His plan for us is that we would constantly be re-created, going "from strength to strength, till [we appear] before God in Zion."[12] There is not a point of arrival, and for some, that may be a relief. While we are alive, we are forever being transformed into the image of Christ. The Word tells us that He takes us *from one degree of glory to another. For this comes from the Lord who is the Spirit.*[13] Each decade, each year, each day, the Spirit will mature us as Christians, developing within us Jesus's heart and mind so that it becomes easier and easier to be His hands and feet.

This requires relying on the Spirit entirely. We will never be able to re-create our lives, so we must commune with the One who can.

A run-in with termites taught me quite a lot about what it means to commune.

My mother ran into the room, looking for me and obviously upset. "Where are they? Where are the pictures of my father?" she said.

She had been looking for something in my guest room so I knew she was referring to the collage that was hanging on the wall. Her father had passed away when she was six years old, and I had had ten photographs of him professionally framed for her. They were the only photographs she had of her father.

"Where are they? The pictures are *gone*!"

I followed my mother into the guest room where she pointed to the empty rectangles in the mat board. All of her father's photographs were just empty spaces. Later we would learn that termites had eaten a hole in the wall and had destroyed the contents of the frame. Two tiny pinholes were the only visible damage in the room. They were smaller than what a thumbtack would leave in the wall. There was so little evidence of the pests, in fact, that one week before, an exterminator had walked through my house for an annual, proactive visit and had not noticed anything out of the ordinary. I had not noticed anything either, but mostly because I hadn't been in my guest room in months, maybe a year. It was always tidy and ready for visitors, so I had just closed the door. *One less room to clean*, I thought.

My inattention to that room had cost a lot. If I had noticed the destruction of the photographs when it began, we might not have lost them all. I learned the hard way that if something is precious, you have to keep your eye on it. If you don't, you could lose it.

When you lose something, you learn what you value most. In my case, I value weekends without housecleaning more than I value a guest room that is perpetually fresh and sparkling. I certainly paid for that choice. Someone else might value a perfectly clean home more than they value recreation. They might pay for that too, but in different ways.

To me, the termites in my guest room were a powerful lesson about something much more important than the maintenance of property. It is about the maintenance of my heart and mind. My attention to or inattention to my inner self determines the quality of my life. I cannot just close the door to certain areas and expect that things will remain as I left them. The scientific truth of *entropy*—that all things break down and decay over time and return to an original state of chaos—is also true of the human personality. God helps keep us in good health by our regular interaction with Jesus. We have to let Him walk through every door in our souls, even the ones that have been closed for a very long time.

In any dictionary, the first definition of *to commune* concerns sharing one's thoughts or feelings with another. The second definition is to receive the sacraments of Communion.

As we explore renewal, let's think of it as inviting Jesus to commune with us inwardly. Let's think of it as accepting Him as a guest into the inner places where we make decisions. But let's also think of it as inviting Him to be our nourishment, of taking Him in as we would the very food that enables and sustains healthy thought. There is a pattern for this nutrition analogy, which is found in the story of the Israelites when they wandered in the desert after fleeing from Egyptian slavery. Though they were in a barren land, God rained manna, or bread, from heaven for their nourishment, leaving it like frost on the lawn every morning. But He also gave them a short list of specific instructions for consuming it. Exodus 16 details these expectations.

1. They were to collect the manna six mornings a week, enough for one day at a time.
2. They were not to keep any of the manna overnight. If they did, it would stink and be filled with maggots when they awoke.
3. They were to gather twice as much manna on the sixth day, so that they could observe the Sabbath rest on the seventh day, when the manna would not fall at all. They were to bake or boil both days' helpings of manna, and on the seventh morning the manna would always be fresh, even though it had been kept overnight.

Those were the three rules. Not too difficult.

"I will test them and see whether they will follow my instructions,"[14] God said to Moses, explaining the simple manna-gathering process.

God was testing the commitment and obedience of His people, but some of them insisted upon testing God. They kept the manna overnight. Yep, maggots. They neglected to go out and collect the double portion on the sixth day. You guessed it, nothing but dry ground on the seventh morning. Though there were only three rules, the people griped and complained that this method of provision was too difficult. They weren't grateful, even though the food was free and fell from the sky. Clearly, God's provisions were not precious enough to keep their eyes on. The Israelites just didn't have time to be bothered with details.

We would have obeyed, we think self-righteously. *We would have handled the manna the right way.*

Are you sure?

Oh, the manna still falls, dear Israelite.

The manna is Jesus. He says,

I am the bread of life. Your ancestors ate the manna in the wilderness, yet they died. But here is the bread that comes down from heaven, which anyone may eat and not die. I am the living bread that came down from heaven. Whoever eats this bread will live forever. This bread is my flesh, which I will give for the life of the world.[15]

Exodus 16 is the representation of how we are to receive our spiritual sustenance in Christ: *every day*. He is the manna; He said so Himself. There couldn't be better—or more humbling—news. The whole time that we have been critiquing the wilderness wanderers of the past, God has been watching us, waiting to see if we would walk out and pick up the nourishment He rains down for us each day in the present. Jesus is the only One who fills our hunger. The Israelites may have received new manna every morning. But we receive new mercies every morning.[16]

This is our everyday genesis.

We can think of the spiritual disciplines as going out to get our Bread for the day. Call it the Manna Model: collect and consume a little every day. Even the same instructions can be applied to our time with Jesus as they were to the Israelites' pursuit of nourishment. The irony of the Manna Model is that the enemy has fooled us into inverting God's instructions.

What did God tell the Israelites to do? His instructions were to gather the bread six days a week and not to gather any at all on the seventh day.

And what do *we* do? We usually neglect the Bread six days a week and try to gather as much as we can on the seventh day. We do this by skipping time alone with God during the week and then expecting to get all the strength we need only at church on the weekend.

According to the Manna Model, the problem that we face is the same one the children of God experienced. When they *did not* gather the manna in the morning, it wasn't there later when they needed it. Whatever manna they happened to leave on the lawn disappeared because "when the sun grew hot, it melted away."[17] In the same way, if *we* do not intentionally spend time with the Lord, we will not have what we need when difficulty arises. Challenges will heat up, and when we turn inwardly for fresh strength, we will find ourselves malnourished. We won't have any faith to draw on. It just won't be there.

But the Manna Model also promises that the blessing we receive is the same one that the children of God experienced as well. When they *did* gather the manna in the morning, "the one who gathered much did not have too much, and the one who gathered little did not have too little. Everyone had gathered just as much as they needed."[18]

Isn't this true for us?

We need to seek God for our daily Bread every morning, but we can stop browbeating ourselves about how we do that.

In the past, the enemy tricked me into neglecting the Bread many times. In fact, let's stop and look a little closer at the way we ingest the Bread: we take in the Word. When I was younger, I would place very high expectations on myself to read the Bible in a certain way, specifically, from cover to cover in one year. With that in mind, I would determine to read the Bible every morning, and if I didn't I would offer myself no grace. I would prescribe a format for myself, a protocol for practicing the spiritual discipline of reading the Word.

Every January 1, I would begin again, opening the *One Year Bible* with an inner vow that I would stick to the schedule . . . or else. By the end of the month, there would be a few days when I had skipped reading, and I would stay up late to catch up. By May, I would have gotten so behind, there was no way I could catch up, so I would quit altogether and purpose to start again . . . *next January 1.* Year after year, I would make my quiet time a chore, as evidenced by its presence on New Year's resolution lists like this:

1. Stop biting my nails.
2. Clean out the garage.
3. Lose 25 pounds.
4. Read the whole Bible.

I would take my eye off what was precious and show what I truly valued in my heart, which was not communion but *completion.* My goal was to complete it—to finish reading the whole Bible. But the Word isn't for accomplishment; it is for nourishment.

The day I truly began to value communion with Christ, everything changed.

Never go a day without consuming the Bread of Life. You find Him in the Bible, not in a Christian-life article or a devotional book, although those are helpful. Read the Bible every day. If you can sit down and read five chapters, great. If you only have time to read one chapter, that's fine. If you only have time to read one paragraph or sentence, then read one paragraph or sentence, but sit down and savor it. It is your daily sustenance. The Manna Model tells us that whether you gather a little or gather a lot, you will have just enough.

Besides, I believe that if you make reading the Bible a priority, something miraculous will happen to you, as it did to me. After all of those years of feeling like a failure ("What good is a Christian who has not read the whole Bible?" I would say to myself), I found release through the Manna Model. I decided to gather what I could. I continued using the *One Year Bible*, but if I skipped a day or two, I did *not* require myself to go back and catch up on the reading. I just bypassed those missed days and stayed on the reading for the current date. If I couldn't read the full portion for that day, I would read just a bit of it. I didn't want to "get it right" anymore. I just wanted to get more of Him.

The spiritual disciplines are supposed to be blessings, not burdens. I hope you hear my heart on that. I want to encourage you to pursue God passionately by multiple methods, but some people might think I'm just adding more to their list of to-dos, or worse, to their list of not-dones. Please do not hear me asking you to do something you cannot do.

Thinking about this reminds me of a story that still makes me cringe, twenty years later. To make a little extra money while I was in college, I decided to host "Camp Cupcake," a one-week summer activity for kids under ten. I advertised at my church, and soon the classes were populated with the eager children of friends and acquaintances. It was going to be fun for all of us, although I took on much more than I should have, which probably doesn't surprise you. I didn't start with one pilot class, no. Even though I had never hosted a day camp before, I arranged to have *dozens* of students moving through my kitchen and living room in shifts.

An overzealous college student, I wanted to make as much summer money as I could by hosting as many classes as I could in the first week of June. In a moment of pride I reasoned, *We are just decorating cupcakes. What could go wrong?*

On the second day of Camp Cupcake, we were going to make a cupcake that looked like it was topped with spaghetti and meatballs made of frosting. The "spaghetti" had to be applied with icing bags. One little class of four kindergarteners was having a bit of trouble squeezing the bags hard enough to get the thick frosting to come out in sweet, pasta-like swirls.

"It won't come out!" they would say.

"Try using both hands to squeeze it," I would answer.

"But I won't come out!"

"Remember to use both hands." Walking to each child, I showed them that putting their other tiny hand on top of their first tiny hand made a difference.

Eventually, they all got it except for one girl, who said again, "It just won't come out!"

"Please use *both* hands!" I answered with emphasis.

This precious girl looked up at me with a puzzled expression and said, "But I only *have* one hand!" It was then that I noticed for the first time that a prosthetic limb peeked out of the end of her ruffled long-sleeved dress. The prosthesis was an odd color and wasn't even functional. It was so obviously fake that once I saw it, it was the only thing I could see.

Her mother chuckled when I told her the story at pickup. But I slapped my forehead and moaned as I said, "I'm so sorry! And why didn't you tell me she was born without an arm? I am so embarrassed that I didn't even notice her prosthesis until the end of the second day! What kind of teacher am I?"

She answered wisely, "I didn't tell you because I have to face the fact that I am not going to be able to pave the way for my daughter everywhere she goes in life. She will have to navigate on her own most of the time. I think it is a positive thing that you didn't notice until the end of the second day. It doesn't mean you are a bad teacher; it means she is a good student. She doesn't focus on what she doesn't have. She has learned to be successful with what she does have."

Oh, that memory. It humbles me. There is a fine line between humility and humiliation. Humility is the thing you could have chosen before humiliation chose you. Humiliation chose me back then. So I am choosing humility today and slowing down to say I love you. It is true. You tend to care for the people you pray for, and I pray for you daily. I wouldn't push you to be legalistic with spiritual disciplines, asking you to "use both hands" when, for whatever reason, you only have one to use. Instead, hear me encouraging all of us with the words of that wise mother: Let's not focus on the time we don't have. Instead, let's learn to be successful with the time we do have.

Lowering my legalistic expectations for myself did not bring about *less* time spent in communion, as I had feared. It brought about more, much more. Not only *more* time, but more rewarding time. More fulfilling time.

I learned something else of spiritual significance from the pest exterminator who treated my home after we found the termites. When I explained my surprise that there was only damage to the photographs and no damage to the wall itself or to the picture frame, he said that he expected as much.

"Pests always take the path of least resistance," he said. "Termites take the easy way. They go for processed wood, like paper, before they go for solid wood."

It made sense. We are no different. When it takes some effort to set aside meaningful time reading the Word, we would just as soon take the easy way. We will read a couple Christ-focused blog posts or a few inspiring status updates—the account of *someone else's* encounter with the Word—and call it a day. We don't stay still and let the very thoughts of God sink into our being. We are satisfied to consume spiritual fast food when we could be sitting down to a feast. Dining on the Word will always take time we don't think we have, but God wants us to take our time anyway.

He wants us to taste and see that He is good.[19] When we taste something sweet, we almost always want more.

As Jesus introduced Communion to His disciples, He affirmed the dual nature of the gift He was giving us through His death. He came to give us the gift of eternal life and the gift of abundant life. Jesus bundles them together, but does not make them inseparable.

For eternal life, Jesus offers His body and says, "Whoever eats this bread will live forever. This bread is my flesh, which I will give for the life of the world."[20]

For abundant life, He offers His blood and says, "Drink from it, all of you. This is my blood of the covenant, which is poured out for many for the forgiveness of sins."[21]

When we take Communion, we celebrate this twofold gift. His body, dying in place of our bodies, enables us to live eternally. His blood, poured out for the forgiveness of our sins, frees us to live abundantly. Our re-creation, our renewal, takes the shape of Bread and Wine. It means we get to live forever and live well. We are charged to consume Communion regularly.

Now look at how Communion connects to Creation.

Communion represents life eternal and life abundant, which

are eerily reminiscent of two of the most important trees God made: "In the middle of the garden were the tree of life and the tree of the knowledge of good and evil."[22] God gave Adam permission to enjoy *almost* everything. "But the LORD God warned him, 'You may freely eat the fruit of every tree in the garden—except the tree of the knowledge of good and evil. If you eat its fruit, you are sure to die.'"[23]

In the Garden of Eden, Adam had eternal life (the tree of life was not forbidden). In the Garden of Eden, Adam also had abundant life (because he communed regularly with God). But God didn't want Adam to partake of the tree of the knowledge of good and evil because He knew it would take away his abundant life. Once Adam knew evil, he would have to die for his sin.

Adam and Eve made a key mistake in that they left themselves unprotected by the armor of God.

They did not wear the belt of truth: they listened to another voice above God's.

They did not wear the breastplate of righteousness: they did not obey God.

They did not wear the gospel of peace on their feet: they made a decision that did not preserve unity with God.

They did not wear the helmet of salvation: they did not pray or talk to God before making the decision.

They did not take up the shield of faith: they did not submit to sound teaching or align the message they had heard with the actual words of God.

They did not take up the sword of the Spirit: they did not turn the question on themselves or ask God to examine their motives before making the decision.

It is no wonder they were vulnerable to the enemy. They were not in communion. As a result, they gave up the abundant life they had in the Garden of Eden. If only they had ignored the tree of the knowledge of good and evil and just kept eating from the tree of life that was right in front of them.

Lack of communion with God leaves us vulnerable to the enemy too. Sure, we may have chosen eternal life when we first believed in Christ to save us from our sins, but it remains a daily question whether we will actually choose abundant life by communing with the One who has saved us.

For Adam and Eve, what was the ultimate result of not wearing the armor of God? Wearing garments of shame instead.

After they followed the enemy's voice, "they suddenly felt shame at their nakedness. So they sewed fig leaves together to cover themselves."[24]

We can put on God's covering or our own. Be aware that the only covering we can make for ourselves is shaped like shame. I keep imagining God on the seventh day, leaning down to look at an ant trying to lift a fig leaf.

"That's too heavy for you to carry," He whispers. "Come to Me and rest."

Like the ant, we struggle onward.

Yet we were not designed to wear or carry shame. Shame will never change us. Feeling bad about the past does not birth a different future. Feeling bad about the life we have been living does not create a new life to live. Our fig-leaf pants look ridiculous on us. It is time to surrender these poorly designed disguises in favor of garments of grace. The Word says to "clothe yourselves with tenderhearted mercy, kindness, humility, gentleness, and patience. . . . Above all, clothe yourselves with love, which binds us all together in perfect harmony. And let the peace that comes from Christ rule in your hearts."[25]

The Spirit is delighted to dress us in royal robes. We are heirs with Christ Jesus, and our lives can be ruled by the peace He has won for us. It is time to stop trying to fix makeshift outfits for ourselves with self-help books and seminars and programs and experts. We don't have to keep eating from the tree of knowledge. Knowing more will not make us more.

For Adam and Eve, there were *two* ways to disobey. They could eat from the wrong tree, or they could *not eat* from the right tree.

We face the same decision every day. The morning sun rises, drenched in new mercies, offering us another chance to make the best choice we can make:

To eat from the tree of life.

Acknowledgments

TREMENDOUS THANKS to Team McDowell, Team Turner, Team Stiles, Team New, and Team Willingham for opening your homes to me as I followed the Lord into new life. You adopted me for a little while, but you will feel like family forever. While I lived with you, I learned how to love.

Thank you to Team Howard for the cabin. And the tires.

Thank you to Team Dodd, Team Lewis, and Team Tucker for letting me borrow your stories as I told my own.

Thank you to Dr. Jon Huntzinger for providing the first feedback and for accepting this manuscript as my master's project.

Thank you to Team Worthy, especially Jeana Ledbetter and Kyle Olund, for polishing and improving this message with me. I trust you so much; thank you for trusting me.

Thank you to Becky Brooks for walking beside me and letting me walk beside you on the path to promises. I am so grateful for Thanksgivings, Wednesday mornings, and ten thousand shared memories. Thirty-three years of laughter is only the beginning.

Thank you to Team Maples for reading yet another manuscript aloud to me, for supporting me in every wild endeavor, and for calling things that are not as though they were. Special thanks to Tara, whose careful feedback and generous ideas were so influential during the initial revising process. You make my writing better. Extra special thanks to Wren, Lily, Shepherd, and Pearl for listening to God with me and for always begging me to tell stories. You make me a better writer.

And thank you to Jesus for rescuing me from myself.

Notes

Introduction

1. Brad Isaac, 2007, "Jerry Seinfeld's Productivity Secret." Lifehacker. http://lifehacker.com/281626/jerry-seinfelds-productivity-secret.
2. Luke 5:31–32 NLT
3. Luke 5:31–32 MSG
4. John 19:30
5. Luke 8:44
6. Philippians 3:12–14 NLT
7. Exodus 20:24–25 NLT, emphasis mine
8. Romans 12:1
9. Malachi 3:6
10. Hebrews 13:8
11. Revelation 1:8 NLT
12. See John 20:19–22 MSG

The First Day

1. Isaiah 43:10
2. Isaiah 41:4 NLT
3. Psalm 14:2–3
4. Romans 1:21, 25
5. Jeremiah 17: 5, 7
6. Matthew 14:25–27 MSG, emphasis mine
7. John 1:1–5 NLT
8. John 1:9–10 NLT
9. Hebrews 13:8
10. John 8:12
11. Psalm 29:3–4 NKJV
12. Matthew 14:30 MSG
13. John 6:63 NLT
14. John 8:12 NLT
15. Hebrews 2:7–9
16. Dallas Willard, "Living a Transformed Life Worthy of Our Calling." Dallas Willard. Accessed November 19, 2016, http://www.dwillard.org/articles/artview.asp?artID=119.
17. Ibid.
18. Revelation 21:5, emphasis mine
19. Luke 15:20 NLT
20. Luke 15:17 NLT
21. Oswald Chambers, *My Utmost for His Highest* (Nashville: Discovery House, 1994), May 19 reading.
22. Howard L. Dayton Jr, *Your Money Counts (Now More Than Ever)*, (Carol Stream, IL: Tyndale House, 1996), xx.
23. Acts 17:27 NKJV, emphasis mine
24. Galatians 3:3 NLT
25. John 6:63 NLT
26. Proverbs 3:5 NLT
27. John 12:24 NLT
28. Romans 8:11, emphasis mine
29. Isaiah 46:13 MSG
30. Isaiah 46:13 NLT, emphasis mine
31. 2 Corinthians 1:20
32. 2 Corinthians 1:20–22, emphasis mine
33. Romans 10:9–10, emphasis mine
34. Romans 10:8–10 MSG, emphasis mine

The Second Day

1. Job 38:22–30 MSG
2. Psalm 148:4–6
3. *Encyclopedia Britannica*, s.v. "Human body," accessed November 23, 2015, http://www.britannica.com/science/human-body.
4. *Encyclopedia Britannica*, s.v. "Atmosphere," accessed November 23, 2015, http://www.britannica.com/science/atmosphere.

5. *Barnes' Notes on the Bible* (http:// biblehub.com/commentaries/barnes /genesis/1.htm).

6. John 1:14 NLT

7. Hebrews 4:12, emphasis mine

8. Ephesians 2:10

9. Exodus 20:17

10. Exodus 20

11. Psalm 32:1–5

12. Psalm 32:5 MSG

13. 1 John 2:16 NLT

14. Genesis 4:6–7 NLT

15. Ecclesiastes 1:8 NLT

16. Proverbs 27:20 NLT

17. Ecclesiastes 5:10

18. 1 Corinthians 10:13 NLT

19. Psalm 77:19 NLT

20. "Henry Cloud | First Conference 2017," GatewayChurchTV, YouTube Video, 47:28, streamed live, January 03, 2017, https://www.youtube.com /watch?v=57zaifYxm0c.

21. Philippians 4:13 NKJV

22. Romans 7:15–20 NLT

23. Romans 7:24

24. 2 Corinthians 4:16 CJB

25. John 3:6

26. Ibid.

27. James 4:17 NLT

28. James 1:14–15 CJB

29. James 1:14–18 NLT

30. John 10:10

31. 2 Corinthians 7:10

32. Galatians 5:25

33. Psalm 55:22 NLT

The Third Day, Morning

1. Psalm 37:23 NLT

2. See Joshua 3:13–17

3. Galatians 2:20

4. John 10:10 CJB

5. John 4:10 NLT, emphasis mine

6. John 4:13–14 NLT

7. John 7:37–39 NLT

8. Colin Welland, *Chariots of Fire*, directed by Hugh Hudson (United Kingdom: Twentieth Century Fox, 1981).

9. Ephesians 2:10

10. Philippians 1:6 NLT

11. Colossians 3:17 NLT

12. Colossians 3:23 NLT

13. Romans 9:20

14. John 4:23–24

15. "What Are Three Categories of Spiritual Gifts?" Institute in Basic Life Principles. Accessed November 19, 2016, http://iblp.org/question s/what-are-three-categories-spiritual -gifts.

16. John 16:13

The Third Day, Afternoon

1. Jeremiah 17:7–8

2. Mark 11:12–14 NLT

3. Galatians 5:22–23 NLT

4. Matthew 11:30

5. John 15:4 MSG

6. John 15:5 MSG

7. Psalm 6:3

8. Psalm 10:1

9. Psalm 22:1

10. 1 Chronicles 12:23–38, emphasis mine

11. 1 Chronicles 12:8 NKJV

12. John 15:7–8

13. John 15:16

14. Proverbs 18:21

15. Ephesians 2:10

16. Psalm 23:1 NLT, emphasis mine

17. 2 Peter 1:3, emphasis mine

18. John 10:4–5

19. John 10:14–16 NLT

20. Matthew 7:15–20

The Fourth Day

1. Psalm 23:4 KJV
2. Jeremiah 29:13
3. Ephesians 3:19 NKJV
4. Ezekiel 37:26 NLT
5. Romans 8:10
6. 1 Peter 1:3 NIV
7. Psalm 22:3
8. Choosing a Bible translation like the NLT that has readable, contemporary language has been outstanding. I relate to it so much more. I use the *One Year Bible* because it is divided in manageable daily portions.
9. Leslie Parrott, *Soul Friends: What Every Woman Needs to Grow Her Faith,* (Grand Rapids, MI: Zondervan, 2014).
10. Oswald Chambers, *My Utmost for Highest* (Nashville: Discovery House, 1994), May 12 reading.
11. Numbers 9:22
12. Psalm 23
13. Matthew Henry, *A Commentary upon the Holy Bible: Genesis to Deuteronomy, Volume 1* (Religious Trad. Soc., 1836), 281.

The Fifth Day

1. Job 12:7–10
2. Romans 1:19–20 NLT
3. Ephesians 2:20–22 NLT
4. Hebrews 10:24–25
5. Judges 7:20
6. 1 Thessalonians 5:11 MSG
7. 2 Samuel 9
8. See Romans 8:38–39
9. Matthew 16:18

The Sixth Day, Morning

1. Psalm 8:3–9 NLT
2. Matthew 11:11 NLT

3. Philippians 2:13
4. Job 26:14 ESV
5. Ephesians 3:20 NLT
6. Hebrews 11:13 NLT
7. John 10:10
8. Romans 8:5–14 NLT, emphasis mine
9. Matthew 6:20–21 NLT
10. 1 Peter 4:11
11. Isaiah 55:11
12. R. R. Johnson, *The Psychological Influence of the Police Uniform* (The FBI Law Enforcement Bulletin, March 2001).
13. John 14:6
14. 1 John 3:7
15. Ephesians 2:14–15
16. 1 Corinthians 2:14–16
17. Romans 10:17 NLT
18. Hebrews 4:12 NLT
19. Romans 12:1 NLT
20. 1 Corinthians 10:31 NLT
21. Philippians 4:8 NLT
22. Philippians 4:6 NLT
23. John 14:1 NLT
24. Proverbs 4:23 NLT
25. Luke 10:19 NLT
26. Romans 12:20–21 NLT
27. Matthew 12:18–19 MSG
28. Luke 4:22 NLT
29. Luke 4:36 NLT
30. Matthew 12:19 NLT

The Sixth Day, Afternoon

1. John 9:6 NLT
2. Romans 8:19 NLT
3. Dallas Willard, "Living a Transformed Life Worthy of Our Calling," Dallas Willard. Accessed December 22, 2016, http://www.dwillard.org/articles/artview.asp?artID=119.
4. Isaiah 28:29 NLT
5. 1 Samuel 16:7 NKJV; Acts 13:22 NKJV

6. See Matthew 22:15–22 NLT (emphasis mine) and Doug Mendenhall, "Whose Image Is Stamped on Your Heart?" (http:// www.huffingtonpost.com/doug -mendenhall/whose-image-is -stamped-on-your-heart_b_5976480 .html).

7. Lamentations 2:19

8. Proverbs 4:23

9. Psalm 51:10 NLT

10. Exodus 17:6 NLT

11. Isaiah 11:4

12. John 7:38 NLT

13. Psalm 119:11

14. James 1:22–25 NLT

15. James 1:17–18 NKJV

16. 1 Thessalonians 5:5

17. Psalm 34:5 NLT

18. Psalm 44:3 NLT, emphasis mine

19. Psalm 34:9–10 NLT

20. 1 John 4:18 NLT

21. Psalm 34:11–13 NLT

22. Mark 10:18

23. James 4:7 ESV

24. 1 Corinthians 11:3

25. Ephesians 5:21

26. 1 Peter 2:13

27. Hebrews 13:17 ESV

28. 1 Peter 5:5

29. Ephesians 5:24 ESV

30. 1 Corinthians 14:34 ESV

31. John 14:10, emphasis mine

32. Philippians 2:13, emphasis mine

33. Romans 8:17 NLT

34. Ephesians 4:29

35. James 3:11

36. Law, William. *A Serious Call to a Devout and Holy Life*. Cornhill: C. Ewer, 1818, 37.

37. Luke 6:45 ESV

38. Exodus 4:10, emphasis mine

39. Hebrews 11:24–26 NLT, emphasis mine

40. Philippians 2:5–11 NLT, emphasis mine

The Seventh Day

1. Genesis 3:8

2. Psalm 121:4

3. Ecclesiastes 3:1–8

4. Isaiah 30:15

5. Colossians 1:15–17 NLT

6. Fenelon, Francois. *Let Go*. Springdale: Whitaker House, 1973, 77.

7. Philippians 4:5–7

8. Psalm 127:2 NLT

9. Exodus 20:8–11 NLT

10. Proverbs 15:23

11. Matthew 11:28–30 MSG, emphasis mine

12. Psalm 84:7

13. 2 Corinthians 3:18 ESV, emphasis mine

14. Exodus 16:4

15. John 6:48–51

16. Lamentations 3:23

17. Exodus 16:21

18. Exodus 16:18

19. Psalm 34:8

20. John 6:51

21. Matthew 26:27–28

22. Genesis 2:9

23. Genesis 2:16–17 NLT

24. Genesis 3:7 NLT

25. Colossians 3:12–15 NLT

About the Author

Nika Maples is a survivor of lupus and a stroke that left her quadriplegic at age twenty. After learning to walk and talk again, she became a public school teacher, winning 2007 Texas Secondary Teacher of the Year. She holds an MA in English Education. When she is not traveling to speak, she lives, writes, and laughs as much as possible in Fort Worth, Texas.

WWW.NIKAMAPLES.COM

Also Available from Nika Maples

HUNTING
HOPE

DIG THROUGH *the*
DARKNESS
to FIND *the* LIGHT

NIKA
MAPLES

ISBN: 978-1-61795-665-2

IF YOU ENJOYED THIS BOOK, WILL YOU CONSIDER SHARING THE MESSAGE WITH OTHERS?

Mention the book in a blog post or through Facebook, Twitter, or upload a picture through Instagram.

Recommend this book to those in your small group, book club, workplace, and classes.

Head over to facebook.com/nikamaples, "LIKE" the page, and post a comment as to what you enjoyed the most.

Tweet "I recommend reading #EverydayGenesis by @NikaMaples // @worthypub"

Pick up a copy for someone you know who would be challenged and encouraged by this message.

Write a book review online.

Visit us at worthypublishing.com

twitter.com/worthypub

instagram.com/worthypub

facebook.com/worthypublishing

youtube.com/worthypublishing